Uncovered

Uncovered

True Stories of Changed Lives

Jonathan Carswell

Authentic

LONDON ● COLORADO SPRINGS ● HYDERABAD

First published 2005 by Authentic Media
9 Holdom Avenue, Bletchley, Milton Keynes, MK1 1QR, UK
1820 Jet Stream Drive, Colorado Springs, CO 80921, USA
OM Authentic Media, Medchal Road, Jeedimetla Village,
Secunderabad 500 055, A.P., India
www.authenticmedia.co.uk
Authentic Media is a division of IBS-STL UK., a company limited by
guarantee (registered charity no. 270162)

British Library Cataloguing in Publication Data

A catalogue record for this book is available
from the British Library

ISBN 978-1-85078-612-2

Some ideas were adapted from {www.life2themax.net} – a website set up by
The Navigators. Used by permission.

Life Times magazine is a publication of Ambassador.
Life Times, Ardenlee Street, Belfast, BT6 8QJ,
Northern Ireland. Phone 028 9045 0010
{www.ambassador-productions.com}

Chapter seven of this book was originally written
by Naomi Billingham but adapted and used with
her permission.

Please note that some of the names, addresses or other personal details
found in this book have been changed.

Cover design by Jonathan Caplin
Print Management by Adare Carwin
Printed and bound by J. H. Haynes & Co. Ltd., Sparkford

Contents

Acknowledgements   vii
Dedication   ix
Introduction   xi

Phil   1
'All my assumptions were blown apart'

Umesh   10
'Hinduism was empty to me'

Kate   23
'Being gay is the way I am'

Nancy   34
'I was there to see justice done'

Howard   42
'My appearance had become my enemy'

Naomi   57
'The lie continued, the mask parade, as my soul dissolved'

Craig   60
'It is unlikely that he will ever walk again'

Nick   69
'They suffered simply for being Jewish'

Adam   78
'Hadn't evolution disproved the Bible?'

Tom   86
'I cannot remember what it is like not to be epileptic'

Eileen   92
'I was a religious hypocrite'

The Truth   98
Jesus said, 'My purpose is to give life in all its fullness'

Further Reading   105

Notes   107

Acknowledgements

The danger in writing the acknowledgements page of any book is that it soon begins to sound like an emotional acceptance speech at the Oscars, thanking everybody under the sun. However, in the months I spent writing this book I have learnt that some things cannot be done without the help of others, and so I want to mention a few of those who have helped me in many different ways.

First of all, thank you to those who agreed to have their stories written in this book. Thank you for being patient with my persistent e-mailing and phoning, asking probing and personal questions.

Thank you too to my family: Mum, Dad, Emma and Ollie, Ben, Hannah and Andy. For all your encouragement, suggestions and support in life and to this book, thank you – I owe you so much. Dad, your input to the book was so helpful, thank you.

Special thanks to: Grandma Carswell, Jo McKenzie, Matt Medlock, Dave Gobbett, Anna Wilkes and my friends on the exec who gave their time to read, proof-read and re-read the book in its early stages in order to shape it to what it is today; at the cost of not watching the BBC2 afternoon film (this applies only to Grandma!), essay-writing, researching for dissertations or watching Wimbledon. Also to Amy, Chris, Andy, Si, Lewie, Nick, Helen and Ed – all of who are great friends and have been consistently there for me.

Ali Hull has been very good to me since we met in the Lake District. Ali, your thoughts and comments on my writing and on this book have been very helpful, thank you.

I am very grateful to my editor, Lucy, who gave me so many helpful suggestions in making this book more accessible.

Finally, Charlotte, Mark and all the staff at Authentic; thank you for enduring my mistakes and fussing – especially for allowing me to re-schedule the deadline of this book so that I could get my essays in on time!

Dedication

For Vinny

Who gave his time and energy to explain and demonstrate to me what it means to be a real Christian.

Introduction

I have lost count of how many times I have shouted 'tell us the truth' at the TV or radio when watching an interview on *Friday Night with Jonathan Ross* or listening to a Radio 1 interview. PR companies who are eager to sell a product have greater control over the celebrities and sports stars than a desire to tell the truth. We are definitely in the age of 'spin' and yet all of us have a desire to know the truth – we hate being lied to or deceived.

This book is the stories of eleven students or recent graduates who have longed to know the truth about the claims of Jesus Christ. All of them are different, all of them are true; all have come to the same life-changing conclusion.

Each person in this book has at some point looked at the claims of Jesus and what they mean in *their* life. It was a totally new concept for some; for others it took months of knowing the facts before they did anything about it. However, all of them have decided that they need Jesus in their life.

You may be living up university life, or struggling to know the relevance of your life – whatever your situation, this book is designed to help you find the uncovered truth.

Jesus said, 'I am the way and the truth and the life. No-one comes to the Father except through me.'[1]
John 14:6.

Phil

'All my assumptions were blown apart'

His parents' car was weighed down with boxes of essentials that he 'just couldn't do without.' Phil had three years of university life ahead of him with perhaps six to eight months of studying caught up in those. He hoped the work wouldn't arrive until at least his second year, if not later. So as this new, more relaxed chapter of his life began, he hit the giant poster sale at the Students' Union in the hope of finding a cheap way to decorate his bland, breeze-block room.

Freshers' Week was over about as fast as it had started and Phil began to settle into university life. He was a pretty open-minded guy, keen to try and experience new things. He joined a few different societies – signing up for things he hadn't known existed, in order to receive a free tea-towel or mug. He drew the line at the sky-diving though – this was a little too extreme. For Phil, university offered opportunities he would never have again, so he was eager to take advantage of them. Along with sky-diving, Christianity was a definite no-no. Christians were nice people who had got things wrong: 'They are just too enthusiastic about their beliefs. If only they spent less time at church praying and reading the Bible, and a little more time enjoying themselves. Christians are far too serious. They're in desperate need of having some fun.'

* * *

The metal railing by the river next to the Union was covered with posters. Phil walked past them most days but his eyes didn't linger long enough to take in what was being advertised – the cold Durham air wasn't kind to those who stopped and stared at advertising. The constant stream of flyers that were being thrust into his hands had become quite tiresome; after all he could not do everything. The Christians on campus were as keen as any one at giving out flyers for their latest event. They were frequently putting on lunchtime or evening talks, always cajoling people to come along.

Despite his perceived ideas and resistance towards all things Christian, Phil went to a lunchtime lecture early in the first year, which tackled the creation/evolution debate. An Australian scientist was speaking on how he believed God was creator of the world.

'Unusually for me, I arrived with plenty of time. Taking my seat close to the back, I whiled away the time by chatting to a couple of friends who were there from my college. I was there for intellectual reasons only. I liked the theory of there being a creator-God, but I wanted to work Him out for myself.'

Exploring Christianity on his terms was appealing to Phil. He was an intelligent guy who thought working out God was like a coffee table puzzle – slightly mind-boggling at first, but given time and thought, the answer would come eventually. The fear that niggled in Phil's mind though was that he was a target for his friends to win over to their way of thinking. 'It was weird. Why were they so keen to brain wash me and bring me round to their way of thinking? They were really nice people on the whole, however when they got into their recruiting mode I wanted to escape – I was not here to be one of their converts.'

Despite going to church in the past and paying some attention in RE lessons, Phil was still unsure of the truth of the Bible. Wasn't it just a collection of unreliable stories written by biased people too long ago to be important?

'My attitude was that while the Bible described the story of a guy who had died – supposedly for me, which seemed very nice of Him, what was the point of it all? Why did I need anyone to die for me anyway? I was doing fine all by myself. **Surely the key to life was not to be over-passionate about Christianity and Jesus, but to enjoy life while we still have it, trying to be good along the way?'**

The Christmas and Easter terms didn't require too much hard work or prolonged thinking, which suited Phil fine, but as the end of second term approached, things changed dramatically. While the work levels stayed pretty low, Phil began to consider some big issues. Emma and Laura, two girls from his college, both Christians, had always been nagging at him, urging him to come to a lunchtime talk run by the Christian Union.

'I had already seen the posters advertising the event before Ems and Lau asked me to go. I was interested in going, although extremely nervous at the thought of going to a talk given by the CU. They were no doubt going to try again to convert me and this didn't exactly excite me!'

Phil sat there looking around the room, trying not to let his nervousness become too obvious. A cold sweat had consumed his body as the speaker was introduced to the expectant audience.

While some of his preconceptions were correct – lunch was not free, this 45-minute meeting demolished Phil's idea that the Bible taught him how to live a good life so he could go to heaven.

'For the first time in my life I realised that actually the Bible talked about how we need to be perfect to go to heaven, something I knew I wasn't.'

'The speaker explained that the Bible said I was going to hell because I had not asked Jesus to forgive me for the wrong things I had done. If I carried on my own way I would have to deal with the punishment myself. But why should I, a fairly good person, go to hell while others much worse than me could go to heaven by asking Jesus to save them? I just couldn't accept that.'

As he lifted his bag from under his seat and headed for the door, Phil's mind was confused.

'Laura, I really don't know what to think any more. I've spent the best part of six months trying to figure out who God is and I am totally confused. All my assumptions and ideas about Christianity have been blown apart. How can God send me to hell but forgive people who are much worse than me?'

It was the first time that Laura had seen Phil take anything so seriously. He had always been the joker in college – the one who played the pranks on others, or started the food-fight in the dining hall. Here he was asking about Christianity!

Phil had picked up an *Identity* book at the lunch bar, which was on his seat when he arrived. It was a section of the Bible, Mark's eyewitness account of Jesus' life.

'When I emptied out my rucksack that night, I allowed the *Identity* book to find its way to the bottom of my cluttered desk drawer. Each time the girls popped round, Emma and Laura would get it out and put it on top of the latest novel I was reading. They kept encouraging me to give the novel a rest for the night and to try and read that instead. "You can only make up your mind when you have actually read it first." I was sceptical though – would reading Mark's biography of Jesus make much difference? After all, I'd studied it for GCSE, and if it hadn't convinced me of Jesus, then why would it now?'

* * *

'Are you coming out tonight, mate? We're going into town. Go on, you've not been out for a while and drinks are two for one tonight at Ikon.'

Phil was seriously tempted. He would have five or six pints most nights, but had slowed down a bit with all the thinking he had been doing recently. 'Perhaps some down time away from my thoughts about God would do me the world of good. Who can refuse a drinks deal anyway?'

It was a great night out. The drinks offer was certainly taken advantage of, but the hangover was now firmly in place; Phil was filled with regret. Yeah, it was fun at the time (well, the bits he could remember), but it was all over now. He was left facing the consequences. Was this really what he wanted? Phil couldn't help but start to think things through again. Not even a big night in town had distracted him from the issues the lunchtime talk had raised.

It was decision time. Could the Bible be trusted? If it was, could he go on ignoring it or would he have to seize the only hope he had – Jesus? He would have to ask for forgiveness from God for the wrong things he had done. Instead of punishment for rejecting God, he would be able to have a real friendship with Him.

As he lay in bed feeling rough and looking much worse, Phil picked up his *Identity* book for the very first time.

'This was not like picking up *The Phantom of Manhattan*; I was not reading this for fun, but rather to see if there was any truth in what it said.'

His eyes poured over each sentence. Surprising even himself, he began to pray: 'God, I don't know if this is true. I don't really know if you are there to hear me. But if you are, show me if this is true.'

This was a huge step for Phil to take. By pleading with God to show him the truth he was setting himself up to be transformed. After all, if the claims made in the Bible were true, Phil was going to have to make a decision – would he believe it or not?

'I still doubted whether there would be any truth in what I was reading but I was actively searching for it.'

He couldn't take his eyes off the page; he was hooked. He was struck by the sheer power and authority that Jesus had in all He said and did. It was just over an hour later that Phil licked his finger, turning to the final page. His headache was wearing off, his thoughts becoming a little less blurry. While millions of questions were fizzing in his mind, a number of them had been answered. What he was reading was true. The evidence was there in front of him and it was so compelling. He had met lots of people who had claimed to have the answer to life but none of them were like Jesus.

'He was different and it seemed as though His claims were true. I came to believe that He wasn't just a man making outrageous statements that He was God, but that He *was* God. It was as simple as that! As I read on, I understood that He wasn't a liar, telling the world a radical message so that they'd take notice of Him, but He was someone telling the truth. Out of love He was pleading with those who didn't believe Him to trust Him, knowing that they'd go to hell without His forgiveness.'

God had answered Phil's helpless cry to show him the truth. As a result, he faced another big choice: either to ask Jesus to forgive him and to live as God intended, or to continue ignoring Him by living for himself. Even after reading the evidence from Mark's Gospel, he still didn't want to choose between God and himself. 'I think **I was worried about what letting God into my life would mean.**'

'This was not a collection of old stories,' Phil remembers, 'rather something which demanded an immediate decision by me: would I ignore God and what Jesus had done for me, or would I ask him to save me? Throughout my life I hadn't just been indifferent to what Jesus had done but I had chosen to block Him out of my life.'

* * *

The bags had been packed for the end of summer term, and Phil was heading home. As he closed his bedroom door behind him Emma was leaving her room and thrust a couple of books into his already full hands. Emma had often given up time to answer Phil's questions about anything religious. She was never too busy for him and always seemed to know the answers. So he thanked her for the books as he set off up the hill towards the station. After showing his ticket to the guard on the platform he struggled onto the train, dropped his bags in the baggage compartment and fell into his seat with an exhausted sigh.

It had been a pretty bad term. Not only had his mind been taken over with questions that had really tough answers, but the four or five pints a night had taken a toll. On top of that was the rejection that had come from a girl he fancied. Things were not looking good. Amidst all of this confusion Phil began to read *Fresh Start*, one of the books Emma had given him.[2] Desperately trying to hide the cover from the other passengers in the carriage, for fear of them realising he was reading a book about Christianity, Phil began to read. His eyes ran hurriedly across the lines and down the pages. Chapter one quickly became chapter four, and chapter four quickly became the final chapter – he couldn't put it down (apart from a quick stop for the loo!).

The message of the book hit Phil between the eyes. It explained very simply how to make that first step of faith, how to become a real Christian. 'This is making complete and utter sense,' thought Phil, 'so what now?'

For the past twenty years of his life he knew he had been doing his own thing, but it simply hadn't worked. If what the Bible said was true, and he believed it was, then he must ask Jesus to forgive him for the wrong things he had done, and ask Him to change him. That evening, after enjoying an evening meal with his family, Phil sat in his room knowing that what he was about to do would change his life forever.

'Jesus,' Phil prayed, 'thank you that you proved to me that the Bible is true. I have done wrong. I beg you to forgive me because I am sorry. Please help me to change. Thank you.'

Phil knew that he could only do one thing – 'I had to live my life with Jesus and for Jesus. Inviting a perfectly loving and good God into my life was the only right thing I could do. I begged Him to forgive me, vowing to live my life for Him.'

Life didn't suddenly become easy. In fact, Phil believes things have got harder: 'The last 18 months of my life have been the hardest months I have ever faced. One close friend who I often went drinking with has found it particularly hard, because I no longer want to go out and get smashed. It is nothing personal, but as a Christian I don't want to live like that any more. We are still good friends, but the change in my lifestyle has affected us. My family have found it hard too. They don't really understand what has happened to me. I was scared to tell them at first. I didn't know how they would react.'

'I was worried they'd think I was strange; getting involved in some sort of cult. I got home at the end of term knowing that I had to say something to them. I was sitting on a bench with my mum, watching a game of cricket at my old school, my palms sweating, when I said, "Mum, I've become a Christian." I sat there, waiting for a response.'

'Mum was no longer worried, but upset. Roman Catholicism meant so much to my parents: my dad had gone to a Roman Catholic church and school. His life was based on Roman Catholicism – but now I was rejecting it. They blamed themselves for not bringing me up as a proper Roman Catholic. It was breaking their hearts.

'I will never forget the day I told them. That evening I got in from church and was greeted with silence from a house that was usually filled with noise and laughter. No one spoke to me. I ate the dinner my mum had kept for me, went up to bed and cried; it was all because of my decision to reject my family's tradition and trust Jesus.'

'Over time dad has gradually come to terms with it. My mum and dad love me hugely and want what is best for me, from their perspective. They want me to find a secure, well-paid job, so that I can be well provided for throughout my life. While that is what I may well end up doing, I want to do whatever and go wherever God wants me – whether that means having a good job or not. They don't want me to get too involved in Christianity, but want me to keep it as a leisure activity. But I simply can't do that: following Jesus as my God and as the Saviour who died for me, comes before everything else.

'My preconceptions of Christianity, the Bible and God have been demolished; there is nothing dull about having the wrong things I have done forgiven. Actually the opposite is the case, because **I have a purpose for the present and hope for the future, and this is amazing!'**

Umesh

'Hinduism was empty to me'

'The chaotic buzz was exciting. It started the moment we stepped off the plane. People were dashing from one place to another, bumping along the crowded roads in their over-loaded rickshaws. Horns were sounding and market-sellers were shouting. It seemed they were trying to make as much noise as they could as they went about their business.'

This was Umesh's first experience of life in India. Along with his Sri Lankan father, he and the rest of his family were there to worship at various Hindu temples, and to take in the sights, sounds and smells of this fascinating country.

'The splendour of the temples was incredible. Everywhere you looked there were bold, striking colours that brightened up the hot and dusty cities. Hundreds of colourful garlands hung round the necks of the countless Hindu idols – placed there by worshippers who were on pilgrimage to pay homage to their gods.'

The golden statues glistened in the bright midday sun, creating quite a sparkle in contrast to the poverty lining the streets. However, the religious glitter that Umesh expected to experience did not happen. Despite the pomp and splendour of the religious journey, the emptiness of it all was now beginning to bore Umesh.

Returning to England three weeks later, Umesh thought through his family's traditions and religious beliefs carefully, concluding that they were not for him.

'Hinduism was so empty to me, and it bored me. The magnitude of the temples was awesome, but at the end of the day they were just buildings. I felt no sense of God while I was there. If I couldn't feel God's presence after all this effort, then the logical response for me was to walk away from it all.'

Something was stopping him though. As part of his school scholarship he was required to sing in chapel every Wednesday and Saturday. If stealing his Wednesday lunchtime wasn't enough, the sheer boredom of the services was. The final straw was when the vicar tried to link his sermons with the latest film releases, and ruined the ending of *The Sixth Sense*. Any respect that Umesh had previously had for the vicar was quickly drained away. Despite being from a devoted religious family, and going to a school that had a highly religious ethos, religion had tumbled from Umesh's life, almost without trace.

And it was with those thoughts that Umesh arrived at university in London. The pursuit of anything religious did not feature in his agenda during this first year. Umesh's thoughts were solely on partying, boozing and scoring a dream goal for the uni football team. As the academic year came to a close, Umesh had passed his exams, partied hard, drunk harder, and yes – he had scored that dream goal as well!

* * *

The first weeks of the summer holidays were a great break from university. Long lie-ins, trashy TV and junk food filled the days (and the stomach); the evenings were generally spent with his best friend and next door neighbour, Ricki. Most nights they could be found in one of three places – playing tennis in the nearby courts, having a drink at the pub or relaxing in Ricki's loft on the PS2.

This summer had been especially hot. Their energy levels had been sapped by the oppressive summer heat, and only four weeks into the summer break they were already desperate for a new activity. Pro-Evolution Soccer had been completed, the controllers looking worn from over-use and Umesh was beating Ricki 6-0 6-0 at tennis more often than not.

'Ricki and I had talked a little about religion in the past, but it was never a topic I had much to contribute to. OK, my family were religious and I had been on a one-off pilgrimage to India, but in my mind that was as far as it went. **I had given Hinduism a go**, mainly out of respect for my family, **and it hadn't worked**. I was prepared to leave all things religious with my failed attempt at Hinduism.'

Using the last of the roast potatoes to mop up the reservoir of gravy that had pooled on their plates, Ricki and Umesh were now allowing their lethargic Sunday afternoon to pass them by. Sundays were always slow for Umesh, whether at university or at home. It was generally a day to finish essays or do some last minute revision before a Monday morning exam. However, the summer holidays allowed for a little more 'down time'. The morning was normally spent in bed as Ricki and his family were at church. By the time they returned home though, Umesh was up and about ready to enjoy a traditional roast dinner – which was usually offered by Ricki's mum.

Aware of Umesh's despondence with Hinduism, Ricki approached Umesh nervously one Sunday afternoon with a question.

'D'ya fancy coming to church with me tonight?'

There was a tone in Ricki's voice that gave the impression he already knew the answer Umesh was going to give. He wasn't hopeful.

'Erm...why? What's happening tonight?' Umesh responded surprisingly.

'Well nothing really. It's a normal Sunday evening service but I thought you might like to come. You've nothing else to do!'

'What time will it finish?'

This was the point at which Ricki thought the excuses were about to come, but Umesh continued to surprise him.

'Are you fobbing me off?'

'No, seriously, what time will it be over? I'll come but I want to be home for *Big Brother* at ten.'

'Ah, you'll be easily home by then. I normally get back for half eight, and that's without rushing.'

'OK.'

'Is that a yes?' Ricki replied in a very excited manner.

'Yes, that's a yes. I'll come to church with you, but it had better be good. If it's like our old chapel services I won't come again. I have heard enough boring sermons in my time!'

* * *

'And this is why I'm not religious,' Umesh thought to himself as he sat on the uncomfortable seat, uninterested and fed up of the sermon. Flashbacks of school chapel services were haunting his mind as the vicar continued to ramble on about the building projects of the Old Testament.

Sitting together, two thirds of the way back from the front, Umesh and Ricki were the only Asians there. As Ricki went each week, this didn't bother him. However, an edge of self-conscious nervousness swept Umesh's body. 'Out of place doesn't begin to describe how I was feeling. I felt exposed – fresh blood in this white, middle-class church.'

During the first song Umesh's nerves did settle down a little as a girl across from him smiled at him. It wasn't just nice to have a pretty young girl smile at him, but it was nice to have some friendly recognition that he was new and unsettled in these unusual surroundings. However, the sermon was long and boring. Umesh was baffled. Why did people allow mind-numbing, pointless religion dominate their lives?

'I couldn't understand how Ricki, as a sensible and lively university student, could be sucked into something so unsuccessful and boring. And yet, despite all I had in my life I had a frightening hole – a hole I couldn't fill. It was a deep cavity that was eating away at my life. I felt I was missing out on something but was unsure what that was.'

However hard Ricki urged and encouraged though, Umesh couldn't believe that Jesus could do something to fill his emptiness. For Umesh, Jesus was a significant prophet or a religious man who was influential to Christians like Ricki, but quite frankly was part of history, and that was all. And if being a Christian meant you had to attend church and persevere through sermons about old buildings from years ago, then he was happy to leave it with Ricki and his family.

Slightly embarrassed at how the Sunday evening service had gone, Ricki decided not to ask Umesh what he thought of it. His opinion was obvious anyway, by the expression written on his face, and the speed with which he wanted to head out of the door. Not a word was mentioned about church again that summer and before long they were loading their parents' cars one more time, heading their separate ways: Umesh to the Guy's, King's and St. Thomas' School of Medicine in London, and Ricki to Oxford.

They kept in touch most weeks either by e-mail or phone, or the odd sneaky text during a dull lecture. They had been best friends and neighbours for sixteen years; they weren't prepared to lose contact despite being at different universities. However, lack of money and busy timetables meant that neither of them managed to get home that term.

It had been eleven weeks since they had had a conversation face to face, but on arriving home, it was as if they had never been away. Before long, they had their tennis rackets out, glad to be back home, enjoying free food and accommodation without having lectures to attend.

However one thing divided them. Ricki was still going to church. Umesh was not. He recognised that there was one big difference between them. 'Despite having great friends, a loving family, and all the possessions I needed, I was unsatisfied and empty. Ricki was not. He claimed it was because he was a Christian, but I was unconvinced.'

With all the catching up that was to be done, their conversation swung on to the Christian Union at Ricki's university, which he was quite involved in. They had had a week of events this last term designed to help people explore the claims of Jesus. Umesh nodded gently asking a couple of questions about the week, out of politeness more than anything else. These were fuelled with a hint of curiosity about what exactly the CU was trying to do, but on the whole they were driven by the fear of offending his friend by not appearing interested.

'Why don't you come to church with me again?' Ricki said a little out of the blue.

'He has clearly got the wrong end of the stick,' Umesh thought, 'I was only being polite when I asked him about the CU!'

'Yeah maybe,' Umesh replied, desperately trying not to commit himself.

'I really think you should, and I promise that it will be nothing like before.'

'Phew, that's a relief! That service I went to last time ranked up there with the most tedious hour of my life, something I didn't want to sit through again.'

It had been a busy Christmas break and the guys had played a couple of matches together, but not spent as much time as normal, catching up and hearing each other's news. Umesh valued the friendship and didn't want this to spoil that.

'Yeah, OK I'll come, but it had better be good. I'm walking out if it's dull.'

'That sounds fair enough. Come round to mine at around 6ish and we'll head down then.'

Umesh looked at his watch as they walked up the steps to the main door of the church – it was 6:29. 'Bang on time,' he thought. They were welcomed by a middle-aged couple at the door whom, judging by the banter, Ricki knew quite well. The couple handed them both an order of service with the announcements for the coming week, and they made their way to some seats on the right-hand side, not too near the front. Sat with them were some of Ricki's friends; guys Ricki had got to know through coming to church.

'I remember being a little surprised (in a good way) with how friendly Ricki's mates were being. This was something I had not experienced from strangers since Freshers' Week! However, their interest in me seemed genuine and sincere. I knew one of them reasonably well. John was the same age as me, with striking blond highlights. He and I had chatted a few times when he had been in the pub with Ricki. I was also surprised at how **the colour of my skin didn't stop them from being friendly**. I don't think I was expecting them to be racist, but Ricki and I were the only Asians there, so I did wonder if we would be seen as outsiders. This was not the case.'

The service went on a little longer than Umesh had hoped – however, it wasn't boring at all. In fact, a couple of songs they sang Umesh knew from school, so he joined in and sang them as loudly as anyone else. The vicar was a middle-aged guy, whom Umesh later learnt was called Steve. 'He was quite a funny looking sort of fellow, someone who you wouldn't take notice of. Unknown to me at the time, what he was going to say that Sunday night was going to change my life forever.'

Steve, like most vicars at Christmas time, was talking about the significance of Christmas – Christmas without the commercialisation, but about the birth of a baby called Jesus. Despite being Hindus, Umesh's family had always celebrated Christmas without really considering the meaning behind it all. As Steve kept talking he began to explain that Jesus didn't come from heaven into this world as a good person who taught good principles of living, but that He came to die.

He continued, 'Jesus' purpose for coming to this world was to enable us to have a relationship with Him. God is perfect, He has never done anything wrong, but as humans we are way below His perfect standard – and that is our major problem. Because God demands perfection, something we cannot achieve, we have fallen short of the mark and we are cut off from Him as a result.'

Umesh was sitting up, listening intently to what was being said. He had talked to Ricki hundreds of times in the past, and it had usually turned into a heated debate.

But despite all the conversations they had had, he had never understood the point of Christianity until tonight, ten days before Christmas.

'If the story of Christianity stopped there, then it would be a morbid and empty story, which would not have impacted billions of people across the world. This is what is so exciting about Christianity – it doesn't stop with the unsettling news of being cut off from the creator of this world, God…'

Steve was getting more and more animated. His hand gestures were becoming more pronounced, his voice bouncing with enthusiasm.

'…Jesus Christ, the baby who was born in a smelly stable was born so that **by dying on the cross, He could bridge the gap between us and God**. He took the punishment for the wrong that each person has done, enabling us to be forgiven by God.'

Umesh was beginning to feel uncomfortable; it was not just because of the seat this time, but because as Steve kept talking Umesh was realising more and more that he was cut off from God; one day he would face punishment for rejecting Him, something that Steve described as a serious consequence.

As Steve spoke, Umesh felt as though his eyes kept falling on him, making what he was saying even more uncomfortable. He began to wonder, 'Perhaps the contentment and peace that Ricki has does actually come from God. It seemed to be making sense. God, who made this world, is perfect. I, on the other hand, have rejected God by going my own way – as a result, the Bible says I am cut off from God. If I keep on rejecting Him I will be punished.'

After the service Umesh got chatting to Paul, one of Ricki's friends. Between sipping a cup of tea and enjoying numerous shortbread biscuits, they relaxed, recalling events of the last term at their separate universities, both agreeing that they had not done enough work!

Without wanting to admit it, Umesh was intrigued by this group of people who called themselves Christians. While Umesh was still feeling like the outsider, he had to admit the innocent but satisfying fun they had was appealing.

Leaving Ricki behind chatting, John and Umesh started to walk home continuing the talk of the last term.

'Mate, is there anything you want me to pray about for you?' John was quite a forward person anyway, but his frankness shocked Umesh who was now frowning a little, out of disbelief.

'Being prayed for? This was a new experience, but being asked for things to be prayed for, I was a little bewildered by the approach.'

'No, not really,' Umesh replied shyly, wishing that either the ground would eat him up or the conversation would move on. Neither happened.

'Yes you do, Umesh, I know you do.'

Normally, Umesh would have responded in one of two possible ways: either he would have shrunk back and gone quiet or given enough time would have snapped, telling John exactly what he thought of his rude, intrusive religious sales talk. This time, he did neither. Instead, Umesh's walk slowed until it came to a stop. He leant against the small sign which displayed the road name.

'John,' Umesh said, looking down to the pavement and playing with the toggle on his university hoodie, 'I want to be part of God's family. I want what you and Ricki have – I want to be forgiven by God.'

The smile on John's face was beginning to broaden. It was exciting for him to see the offer of Jesus' forgiveness impact Umesh's life. John was more than a spectator. He and Ricki had spent years explaining to Umesh the claims that Jesus made; he was now asking Umesh for things he wanted to pray about.

'You can have all this – you know you can.'

'Yeah…I know…but…'

'What? But what?' John replied, slightly impatiently, but with excitement, not wanting Umesh to suddenly be taken over with doubts.

There was a further pause, neither of them saying a word. The frown on Umesh's forehead was speaking volumes. There was something holding him back.

'Is it your family?'

'Yeah, yeah it is,' Umesh replied as though he was relieved that John had guessed.

'What are they going to say?'

'They're going to take it personally, and it's not personal. They believe in Hinduism, but I know it's empty. I know the only answer is Jesus – forgiveness from God.'

Umesh still had a few questions buzzing around in his head. The longer he talked with John though, the more he began to work the answers out for himself. This was going to be a step of faith for Umesh – he feared his family would react badly, wondering how he would cope as a Christian at uni. He was travelling back for the spring term that night!

'Umesh, **the question you have to ask yourself is "Is Christianity really true?"** And if it is, is it worth the difficulties? If you don't think it is then you're worrying yourself unnecessarily, but if it's true then…'

'…then I have to trust God, whatever the consequences,' Umesh interrupted, finishing John's sentence. He knew it was true, but letting God transform your life was not a small decision to make. Letting go of living under your own rules is not something that happens easily.

'Yeah, that's right. Umesh, you know it all, what's stopping you?' John said with a slight smile. He didn't want to rush him, or make him do something he didn't want, but sensed that Umesh needed a little nudge.

'Nothing I guess…'

They both looked at each other and laughed, relieved at being able to let out some nervous energy.

'What should I say when I pray for Jesus to forgive me? I just want to tell Him I'm sorry; that I want to change.'

'Tell Him that then!' John said with animation. 'Because Jesus' death is totally sufficient to wipe out all the wrong things that someone has done, all we need to do is recognise that only He can forgive us, ask Him to do that and He will. We cannot change ourselves, but because He is the all powerful God, He can change us. It's really exciting.'

'Yeah I know…'

Umesh's head was still bowed as he began to pray, quietly. John had to strain to hear what Umesh was saying as the traffic from the road was drowning him out a little.

'Jesus,' Umesh began, 'I am sorry I have messed up my life by living for myself. I am sorry. Will you forgive me? I know that you are perfect and that's why I want to say sorry – I want to change and be more like you. Please can you help me do this? Thank you.'

Umesh looked up at John. For the passers-by in their cars, nothing dramatic had happened. However, for Umesh, the last twenty seconds had been the most significant and spectacular in his whole life. He knew he was now a Christian, forgiven by the perfect Creator of this world – God.

* * *

Since Umesh became a Christian, he doesn't regret this momentous decision for one minute, despite the response of his family.

'The way my family reacted was worse than I had expected. They were outraged that I could turn my back on Hinduism and are by no means complimentary about my new found faith. **It is the best decision I have ever made** though. It has transformed my life and I am keen to tell everyone about how Jesus has transformed my life.'

Kate

'Being gay is the way I am'

Kate arrived at the University of Kent certain of two things: she was gay, and Christianity was not true.

From her early teens she knew she was gay. It wasn't a deliberate choice that she had made, and it wasn't a feeling or emotion that had developed over a period of time either. As Kate says, 'It was the way I was... As soon as I started to be aware of any sexual feelings, I knew I was gay. It took me a little while to understand what it actually meant, but I think that is the case with any teenager on an issue like this.'

Kate's perception of Christianity came a little time after this when reading a short sentence in the little red Bible she had been given on starting school. While sat at her desk one time, trying to avoid her homework, she picked the book off the shelf and started to read small sections. She was interested to see what it said on various topics and it wasn't long before she stumbled across a sentence that contained the phrase 'homosexual offenders'.[3]

She read the sentence a second time checking each word carefully, and on realising she had read it correctly she shut it tight and threw it towards her bed with some disgust. 'Homosexual offenders?' she thought, 'How could a God of love say that? After all **God must know that I haven't *chosen* my sexuality**. Being gay is the way I am. This cannot be the Word of God as Christians claim – it is a set of rules set by ignorant, narrow-minded people.'

* * *

On the first day of university one of the first people Kate met, while registering for her music course, was Stella. A Christian. Like a lot of people, Kate had presumed that Christians such as Stella were goody-goodies, who were so stuck into reading their shiny covered Bibles that they were totally oblivious to the world around them; so caught up in church and God to ever have fun or even have a sensible, intellectual conversation.

Stella was intelligent, fun and down-to-earth and before long the two girls became very good friends. For Kate though, there was one problem. 'How could a bright student like Stella read and believe something as ridiculous and out-dated as the Bible?'

At this stage Kate had kept her sexuality a secret but wondered what her friends would think if they knew. What would Stella think? Would she still be friends with me? Would she treat me differently? Would she start telling me I was wrong? Questions like these would fill her mind. 'When I got drunk,' she recalls, 'I would start asking her questions about what she believed, a little out of interest; but mainly trying to sound her out subtly about the homosexuality issue.'

The next morning Kate's memory of the conversation the night before would be a little hazy from one too many Jack Daniel's and cokes; but over the course of the first two terms Stella somehow managed to get across to Kate that while yes, the Bible does say homosexuality is wrong, it is referring to the *act* rather than the orientation of it. This was a vitally important distinction for Kate, as she could do something about one but not the other.

'What Stella was saying was that it was possible to be a Christian and gay – but you were to remain celibate. Either way, I found what she said deeply offensive. The idea that what I wanted to do sexually was somehow sinful seemed outrageously unfair, and **I carried on constructing my convincing arguments against Christianity**.'

Kate continued to question Stella about her beliefs, still amazed that an intelligent adult could be sucked in by what the Bible said.

'I pressed her on issues that didn't make sense to me. She was getting more involved with the CU and was encouraging me to go along to events that they were hosting. If I'm honest it was giving me food for thought but it was by no means convincing me. In fact, I felt a little embarrassed for Stella and her friends. To be at university, and to be talking about Jesus seemed to me to be very sad.'

Halfway through term there was an event being hosted by the CU in one of the colleges on campus – the title was 'Who is Jesus?' Stella had asked Kate to come a couple of weeks earlier but received the usual, non-committal response of 'maybe'. It was the day of the event and Kate was wandering towards the canteen, trying to fill the gap between her midday and early afternoon lecture, when she bumped into Stella. After a couple of minutes of banter, Stella asked Kate if she was busy and if she wanted to come to the CU event. Unable to think of a suitable excuse quick enough, Kate was soon on her way to the talk with Stella by her side. The two chatted as they approached the hall where lunch was being served for the talk.

Kate knew a few of the guys from the CU as a result of her friendship with Stella, and upon her arrival they fixed her up with some lunch and made her feel quite relaxed with the situation. However friendly they were though, Kate was still agnostic, cynical and even offended by the concept of there being a God.

She left the talk that afternoon, heading for her music composition lecture, still cynical but with niggling and nagging questions hanging over her mind: 'Was Jesus mad? His life didn't seem to point to the conclusion that He was mad or evil. He claimed to be God and did all kinds of amazing things, which, as the speaker pointed out, were recorded by regular historians as well as the Bible writers.'

Kate could not argue Jesus out of the equation. There was too much she couldn't explain. 'As far as Stella was aware though, I was still as aggressively anti-Christian as I had ever been. She was right I guess, because I had absolutely no intention of becoming a Christian, and so I neglected the nagging thoughts I had, and carried on enjoying living the typical student lifestyle.'

* * *

Halfway through Kate's second year, Stella told her that she wanted to have a chat. She looked serious and a little bit nervous, but Kate agreed, and the following day they met up in Kate's room.

'Kate,' Stella said, looking even more nervous than she had been when she'd asked to meet up, '**I know that you're gay and I want us to be open about it**.'

Kate obviously hadn't been as subtle as she thought in her drunken conversations, but she was delighted. 'A feeling of relief washed over my body as the fears of

Stella not wanting to be my friend if she knew about my sexuality were not realised.'

However, after a few days of chatting openly about her feelings and what she hoped for in a relationship, Kate became aware of Stella being a bit funny about it all. It was now Kate's turn to invite Stella for a serious chat.

'I confronted her about the way she was acting around me and waited for her response.' She explained that although she was my friend, and accepted me as I was, she could not condone me for having a homosexual relationship. Stella explained that she believed the Bible said homosexual relationships were wrong and so if they were wrong she couldn't compromise on it – the Bible said it, she believed it and so therefore, in her mind, that settled it.'

While hoping not to offend, but being seriously blunt Stella spelt out exactly what she believed.

'Kate, whether you are straight or gay, you are not living in a way which pleases God, and the Bible says this has serious consequences. It says to everyone that the result of rejecting God is death, punishment in hell. However, **God gives eternal life to anyone who believes** in Him as a result of Jesus' death on the cross. You have a big decision, with two options leading to two different consequences.'

And on that note they ended their conversation and the two girls went their separate ways. Stella hoped that she had not been too blunt with Kate and as a result was going to lose a good friendship, while Kate was left sitting on her bed, struggling to get the thought of God's punishment out of her head.

The next morning, while sipping a strong black coffee, Kate sat on her bed and began to write:

Stella,

I wanted to speak to you, because I needed to know that I had your support on this and I needed to feel I could talk to you about it. Now I feel even less comfortable with it – in fact completely *un*comfortable, because now I know you are always judging me. You can never be happy for me when I have a relationship. I can't talk to you about it because you think it's wrong. It's not enough for you to say you're fine with it as long as I don't act on it. I don't feel I can go to you for support, because I don't feel supported by you telling me I am going to hell. If being open with you is going to mean I'm going to be preached at, then I don't need that. That doesn't help me – it makes me feel ashamed. I don't know what this means for our friendship now. If you can't accept me, we're not going to resolve this.

Your way gives me two choices. Either I throw my life away for God, or I embrace my life and get punished in hell. If that's the case, I can selfishly say that I am not prepared to live my life in any way except for myself, and the people I love.

I'll see you around,

K

'I can't imagine how Stella felt receiving this; I can only imagine she must have given up on me. But the fact is she had planted thoughts in my mind that would not go away. I still could not explain who Jesus was, and there must have been a part of me that wondered if God really existed; a part big enough to realise that if hell existed, I was heading there, and to make me scared of what that

might mean. I was finding it harder and harder to squash
these kinds of thoughts, and so instead I actively began to
read books that claimed to disprove the Bible and talk to
people who didn't believe it all, to try and make it all go
away.'

* * *

Despite the letter, Stella was surprisingly relaxed about it
and their friendship continued. As the new term started,
Stella managed to persuade Kate to go along to a week of
talks that was being hosted by the CU.

'As I listened to the talk each lunchtime, I was seeing
all of my carefully constructed arguments against God
being shattered. The final talk of the week, on Saturday,
had the title "Jesus: No one forgets a good teacher?"'

If Kate was honest, she was nervous about going. She
had no solid argument against the God who Stella said
was the God who made and loved her, but hated the
wrong things she did. 'That afternoon the speaker was
talking about an incident in Jesus' life that shocked those
that were there,' she remembers. He read the account of
the paralysed man from Mark's Gospel:

> Several days later Jesus returned to Capernaum,
> and the news of his arrival spread quickly through
> the town. Soon the house where he was staying
> was so packed with visitors that there wasn't room
> for one more person, not even outside the door.
> And he preached the word to them. Four men
> arrived carrying a paralyzed man on a mat. They
> couldn't get to Jesus through the crowd, so they
> dug through the clay roof above his head. Then they
> lowered the sick man on his mat, right down in front

of Jesus. Seeing their faith, Jesus said to the paralyzed man, 'My son, your sins are forgiven.'

But some of the teachers of religious law who were sitting there said to themselves, 'What? This is blasphemy! Who but God can forgive sins!'

Jesus knew what they were discussing among themselves, so he said to them, 'Why do you think this is blasphemy? Is it easier to say to the paralyzed man, 'Your sins are forgiven' or 'Get up, pick up your mat, and walk'? I will prove that I, the Son of Man, have the authority on earth to forgive sins.' Then Jesus turned to the paralyzed man and said, 'Stand up, take your mat, and go on home, because you are healed!'

The man jumped up, took the mat, and pushed his way through the stunned onlookers. Then they all praised God. 'We've never seen anything like this before!' they exclaimed.[4]

'I remember the talk as if it was yesterday. The speaker emphasised the point that there are lots of things in life that we *want*, but there is one thing that we all *need* – forgiveness. I realised for the first time that however desperately I wanted to be in a relationship with a woman, I had a far greater need for God's generous forgiveness to save me from hell.'

Kate excused herself quickly from the meeting and rushed home, ignoring the tempting offer of jam doughnuts that were at the back of the hall. The rush past the sugary doughnuts was noted by Stella – something must have gripped Kate's mind!

She arrived home nearly ten minutes later and sat down heavily on her bed allowing tears to flow uncontrollably down her cheeks. **'I want to be forgiven**. I want God to forgive me,' she thought, almost mouthing the words, such was her desperation. She knew, from attending so many of the CU events, that she needed to ask God for His forgiveness; asking too that He would change her and help her live for Him rather than herself. This is what she did, tears still flooding her eyes.

> 'God, I'm sorry. I want to be different; I want you to change me. Thank you for dying in my place, taking my punishment, so that I can be forgiven. Please forgive me from all the wrong things I have done. There is so much I have done wrong, but I know that you are big enough to forgive all of them. God I feel so weak and know that I am still going to mess up so please don't expect me to be perfect, but please help me to be more like you. I know that you will hear and answer this, so thank you.'

After two and a half years of putting off and shutting out all that Stella had been saying Kate finally became a Christian.

* * *

That night, as she lay in bed, a thousand and one new thoughts were running through her mind. She knew that her life was going to be different now she was a forgiven person, doing her utmost to live for God. Kate knew, from what Stella had explained to her, that being a homosexual Christian meant she was facing a life of celibacy. She opened her red Bible for the first time since she had stumbled across the phrase 'homosexual offenders' all those years ago, and began to read from Psalm 34:

> The eyes of the LORD watch over those who do
> right;
>   his ears are open to their cries for help.
> But the LORD turns his face against those who do
> evil;
>   he will erase their memory from the earth.
> The LORD hears his people when they call to him
> for help.
>   He rescues them from all their troubles.
> The LORD is close to the broken-hearted;
>   he rescues those who are crushed in spirit.
> The righteous face many troubles,
>   but the LORD rescues them from each and every
> one.[5]

As she read it she knew that God was saying that yes, the
path ahead for her was one that would be tough, but He
would be with her every step of the way. In the same way
that He heard her cry for forgiveness, He would hear her
and help her every time she cried to Him in the future.

* * *

'Looking back to the night I became a Christian I can
honestly say that the days, weeks and months that have
followed have probably been the hardest I have ever had
to face. All of my hopes and ambitions for the future had
been based around settling down and being happy and in
love with someone. It was incredibly difficult to adjust to
the prospect of a life of singleness and celibacy, and for a
time, I found it unbearable to watch romantic films or
listen to love songs. I was acutely aware of my sexuality,
and its pull away from God was incredibly strong at
times.

'I eventually met and fell in love with a woman, and had a brief and tortured relationship with her, being aware all the time of how much I was hurting God and damaging my relationship with Him. In the end I chose God, and it was not until I began to really seek Him, that I began to taste the sweetness of what it means to be loved and saved by God. Getting over my relationship meant being uncompromising in my thoughts, with the people I spent time with and in my attitudes to my future and my singleness. I discovered that as I endeavoured to be obedient to God in *every* aspect of my life, I began to experience the peace and joy that I had so often read about in the Bible.'

Kate realises that her identity is not in her sexuality or her personality but God alone. 'I have begun to understand that God loves me as an *individual*, not just as part of a corporate whole, and that He has given me unique gifts to serve others. It is in this service that I find an amazing peace and joy that makes being a Christian such an awesome and enviable thing. God had loved me the whole time, but it took me a while before I moved away from my own desires long enough to see that.'

Although Kate still struggles every day to make the right choices in the small things as well as the large, she realises that God has stuck to the promise that she read the first night she became a Christian. 'He *has* heard me every time I have cried out to Him, and I know He will continue to do so every day until I die and go to heaven, where He promised to wipe away every tear from my eyes.'

Nancy

'I was there to see justice done'

Nancy arrived at Durham University just as the autumn leaves were falling onto the riverbank. The picturesque city looked radiant as a fresh wind skipped through its steep, cobbled streets. The years ahead filled her life with excitement, not necessarily for the studying, but the opportunities and experiences that university presents. To any onlooker, Nancy was a normal student, with an extra helping of enthusiasm and fun. However in Nancy's past lay a series of events that had changed her life forever.

It all started when the local paper reported: 'Headmaster Suspended'. Pending an inquiry, the paper explained, the headmaster had been suspended from the school and was on police bail following allegations of sexual abuse from several pupils, past and present. With any investigation like this a helpline had been set up for worried parents. Nancy's mum was one of the first to call as Chris, her brother, was now attending the school. Was he in any danger?

The court tape was rolling and the transcriber was furiously punching at her keys. Nancy had heard about court video link-ups for those who were too young to appear as witnesses, but she had never seen one, let alone been in one herself. As she sat there rigidly, the first face she saw was that of the judge.

'Nancy?' he said.

'Yes.'

'Good – just wanted to check we could hear each other. In a moment you will be asked a few questions by Mr Harris QC. Is that OK? You have as much time as you want. We need to understand your version of what happened,' he said with a smile.

'O-OK,' she replied nervously.

I was there as a witness – a witness for the Crown who were prosecuting my former headmaster. The judge told me a little more about why I had been asked to answer questions via this video link, explaining that my former headmaster was facing numerous accounts of sexual assault and one charge of indecent assault. Faced with the charges he had pleaded 'not guilty'.

Not guilty! My blood began to boil. How could he be not guilty after all he had done? For seven years he had abused me and other girls at the junior school and now he dared to claim his innocence.

I was fourteen at the time and it was not an easy thing to deal with, not because I was a shy, withdrawn teenager, but because my former headmaster was also a member of the small church I attended at the time.

My mum knew that things at school were not as they should be. In my more emotional moments I had tried to explain the incidents that had gone on, but had begged her not to say anything to anyone and, rightly or wrongly, she agreed. It was while she was on the telephone to the helpline that she mentioned that I used to attend the school – and that's when the police became interested. My mum happily volunteered my services to give a statement on what had happened during my time there. After getting over my initial annoyance that mum hadn't asked me first, I agreed that I would. After all, it might help me put an end to it all and move on.

It was about eighteen months later that we received another call from the police. They believed that they had enough evidence to charge and prosecute – was I willing to testify in court? I had originally promised myself that I would never say anything about it to anyone again, no matter what. It had been a horrible time of my life, I certainly didn't want to start trawling it up again. However, I changed my mind. The stubborn streak that normally ruled, gave in. Anything to reveal the truth, anything to see him put away. I was going there to see some justice done.

Bitterness towards my former headmaster had multiplied, so that by now I hated him. I wanted the opportunity to give an account of the wrong done against me, but was aware that away from court my story had stirred reaction. The majority of my church couldn't believe that this good man could have been involved in such a crime, so I became nervous and unsure as to whether I should give evidence at all. I was only a young schoolgirl, and how people saw me mattered. If those at church wouldn't believe me, why would they in court?

It took just under an hour for the defence and prosecution to finish their questioning. I hadn't held back in my responses. The questioning was intense and persistent, and so I was pleased when the judge thanked me and the video link was stopped. The policewoman who had sat next to me throughout, led me out to the lobby where my mum and dad were waiting for me. I was so relieved it was all over. We had not talked about the abuse or the trial during the months leading up to it. The journey home was no exception. I learnt this was not an issue to be discussed.

The trial lasted just over a week. The accused was sentenced to eighteen months in a high security jail. He served just nine months. Before I knew it, he was back, sitting only a few rows in front of me at church. Cold sweats consumed my body as I watched him stroll into church week after week as if nothing had happened. It was then that I decided **going to church was not for me**. It was full of hypocrites who were no different from everyone else.

In town, I found myself diving into random shops as I saw him on the other side of the high street. Apart from that, life progressed as normal, or so it seemed. Inside I was angry, hating, and highly irritated by life. The few friends I had were rapidly drifting away due to my temper – a temper I couldn't control. I didn't know how I could escape my own problem. I was trapped. The counsellor at school, whom I was told I must see, was of little help. Each week she told me, 'You will never get over this trauma.' Great, I thought, what a prospect! This was not what I wanted to hear. I was not prepared to let this man's crime affect me forever. How I was going to do this though, I had no idea.

* * *

Before I knew it I was in year 11. Without wanting to sound like an old woman, I don't know where the years went. At the end of year 10 I had become close friends with a guy at school. Why he liked me I have no idea. I was horrible, but Andy cared for me, loving me as no other friend had. It was an added bonus that he was rather sexy! We were inseparable, doing everything together. He went to a new church down the road from me; one I didn't even know existed. It was about a year after we first became friends that he asked me along to a youth night. I hated God because in my mind, He had let the abuse happen, but Andy *was* quite sexy, so I agreed to go with him.

It was so different from the little church I had been to before. For starters, everyone was happy to be there. From my experience of church, people only went because it made them feel better, so they could tick the imaginary religious box for another week. To my surprise, I enjoyed this new church. My anger still consumed me though. In my mind, the notion that God was great and mighty seemed impossible. If He couldn't stop a sick head-master, He couldn't be that big.

The next day Andy went on holiday for a couple of weeks. I was at a loose end as he was my only friend. I drove mum mad messing around at home! The following Sunday, mum was unusually enthusiastic for me to go to church. I had been a bit of a handful during the week, so she was keen to have me out of the house for an hour or two. Before I knew it I was putting my coat and shoes on, closing the front door and making my way towards the church I had been to with Andy.

I went back week after week for about a year and, believe it or not, I actually had a lot of fun making new friends. There was something different about them. I knew exactly what it was. Each week they banged on about the importance of being in a relationship with Jesus – He had changed them. However, I continued to refuse to alter my attitude towards God. My stubbornness, which had controlled me ever since I could remember, still gripped me, holding me back from seriously considering God.

Things changed forever on December 17th. I had been involved in the planning and preparation for the youth Christmas service, even helping with the 'God' bits of the programme. I was such a hypocrite in doing so, but enjoyed the company, and so was carried along with it all. I was on the back row of church, slightly hidden by the stone pillar. The service was going well, including the parts I had contributed to. The vicar was concluding with a talk about Christmas and its relevance for today. I usually listened to the first couple of minutes of his talk as he started with a story, but after that I normally stared out of the window and day-dreamed.

For some reason, **I didn't stop listening this time. I was gripped**. I began to understand for the first time that God *did* love me. The vicar was being pretty blunt. He talked about the wrong in people's lives – things that we never worry about, but deep down know are wrong. It was as though he was talking straight at me. I knew that the anger and hate I felt were wrong. The way I had treated people wasn't right either. He went on to explain how much of what I was doing hurt God. It was cutting me off from Him and I deserved His judgement. However, because He loves us so much, He came to this earth to give us a rescue option. Christmas reminds us of the start of His rescue operation.

The hairs on the back of my neck were standing on end. It was as though a huge weight was being taken from my shoulders as the realisation of what Jesus had done for me began to dawn in my mind. I fought back the tears. It had taken me over a year to understand how much I needed God, but I was still apprehensive about admitting that I had done wrong. It would leave me so open and vulnerable, a feeling I knew so well. I knew I couldn't go on, I had to be honest before God.

The vicar, as he began to finish, explained that what we need is to ask for God's forgiveness for our deliberate wrongdoing, asking Him to help us change so that we can live for God. He said a prayer slowly so that those who wanted to ask God to forgive them could pray after him, one line at a time.

Very quietly I began to pray, repeating each line of the prayer. We used to pray every morning at junior school, but I had never done it out loud before, fearing that someone might actually hear. I knew I had done wrong to others, but ultimately I had done wrong against God and so I needed His forgiveness. The vicar explained that the words he was praying were not specially set out in a ritualistic form, but rather it was their meaning that was significant.

Frost was beginning to form on the ground as I left the church. For the first time in my life I felt contented. I must have looked quite strange as I smiled to myself!

'Hi, I'm home,' I bellowed, as I hung my coat up in the hallway.

'Nancy? Is that you?' my mum called back. 'What's got into you? Why are you *so* cheery?'

Normally when I got in from being out I would immediately dump my bag in the hall and dash up the stairs two at a time into the safety and comfort of my room – not so today.

The conversation we had next is one I will never forget. Mum and dad were in the kitchen chatting over a mug of hot chocolate as I began to explain what had happened at church that evening. My parents listened politely as I bounced around the kitchen, trying to get me to stand still for a moment. Throughout my childhood they had wanted me to be religious, but this was not what they had in mind. They thought I'd been sucked in by a random wacko cult group – when in fact it was an ordinary, mainstream denomination. It was so different from what they had expected.

As I read the Bible I learnt that if I asked God to forgive me, I needed to forgive others too, no matter what they had done. I struggled with this for weeks and months. How could I forgive my headmaster for all he had done?

Only through understanding all that God had forgiven me for. **God's forgiveness allowed me to forgive my former headmaster**.

The Bible says that, 'If you confess with your mouth, "Jesus is Lord", and believe in your heart that God raised him from the dead, you will be saved.'[6] That even includes my former headmaster.

Howard

'My appearance had become my enemy'

What I saw in the mirror I hated: my nose, my hair, my eyes. Catching a glimpse of myself in a mirror or in the reflection of a CD filled my mind with disgust at how I looked. If this was how I was thinking, what were the girls in my A level classes thinking? They must have hated me as much as I did if not more, or so I thought. Not that I was scarred or disfigured in any way. I just wanted to change. I had a low self-esteem. I wanted my physical appearance to bring me happiness and I was prepared to do anything to make that happen.

For the average passer-by everything in my life would have seemed fine. I was part of a happy and loving family who had enough money for it never to be an issue. I got on well with my sister, Sarah, too, despite the age gap. It all seemed so perfect; however, inside I was desperately struggling.

To me the world was futile and meaningless; my small existence was counting for nothing. Only those who conformed to the notion of beauty were accepted. I didn't count myself to be in this category and so felt that I could never be happy. **I wanted what others had – the good looks, which I believed brought success and happiness**.

Some people think religion is the answer – that was not what I thought. I thought Christians were insecure, naïve and belonged in a mad house. They believed in a man-made self-help tool, born out of a time of crisis and suffering. All of this was intellectual suicide. Religion was not going to provide any answers for me, or so I thought until I arrived at university where I met two people who squashed my thinking for good.

* * *

I had toyed with the idea of plastic surgery for some time. 'Plastic surgery is the answer,' I thought. 'If I have a small change here and there, I'll be happy.' In short, my appearance had become my enemy. I believed that the only route to happiness was to look good. I was prepared to make this happen at whatever cost.

Naturally, my parents were worried about me. I had, in the previous few months, become quite reclusive. I stayed in my room a lot of the time, unenthusiastic about going out with my mates. It was as if I had put my life on hold until I was satisfied with my appearance. My school work didn't suffer, as staying in gave me time to work, but my friends had become somewhat distant.

Aware that I was toying with the idea of plastic surgery, my parents suggested I should see a doctor or somebody professionally qualified in this area before rushing into anything. I happily obliged. If anyone could help me, I was willing to listen to their advice. My mum arranged for me to see my GP a couple of days later. When the day of the appointment arrived we went to speak to him together about the suggestion of having plastic surgery. I was referred to a NHS doctor at first but was soon transferred to see a private plastic surgeon, Dr Gault. He was caring and sympathetic to my situation. He could see how insecure I had become as I struggled to make eye contact with him. He was mildly confident however, that he could improve my appearance. However, he was also very honest about the whole thing.

'Howard, at the end of the day, it is your decision and I am not going to stop you from having it done. However, I do want you to understand that plastic surgery is a temporary fix. It may help for the short term, but it does not solve anything. It doesn't change you as a person.'

I wasn't listening. My mind was set on having surgery because I could see no other way to be happy. I was desperate. No matter what other advice I received, it fell on deaf ears.

Mum and dad were not supportive of the idea, but because of their love for me, my obvious loneliness and despair, and because of the confidence they had in Dr Gault, they agreed. So a date for the operation was set, and in the summer holidays between lower and upper sixth form, I had a nose and ear job.

They were distraught, but in contrast I found my excitement hard to contain. The prospect of being fixed was electrifying. I thought this was the beginning of a brand new me. The wheeling into theatre was an exhilarating experience. I was taken over with the thoughts that in a couple of hours I would be leaving, slightly sore, but looking pretty good and feeling happy.

As I lay in the hospital ward post-surgery, my face was numb and heavy. They said it would be, but this was unreal. I was still wearing a tight mask they had fixed over my nose and I felt like there was a ten tonne weight pressing on my face. 'It will all be worth it though' I told myself, 'if it makes me look good. A couple of days of pain are worth persevering with if it brings years of happiness and contentment.'

Eating was difficult but laughing was near impossible. Jokes were not allowed – the pain of smiling was too much! It was exciting though: how would I look when the mask came off and the bruising had died down?

When I looked at my reflection in the mirror for the first time since the operation I got a shock. I had thought that I would struggle to recognise this new face that I was seeing – instead it was basically the same old face I had always seen.

Nearly two months had passed since the operation and I was now back at college. None of my friends were aware that I had had any surgery. Whether or not they noticed, I have no idea. It was when I was getting ready one morning that I caught myself in the mirror. As I pulled my jumper over my head, I looked disconsolately at the reflection of myself in the mirror. I was still dissatisfied with how I looked.

I wanted more surgery. My heart was heavy with the emptiness that my life had thrust upon me. **I had hit rock bottom**. I sought an escape but found none. I was trapped in my own self-despair. I was unhappy and unsatisfied; empty and longing for a purpose to my life. It was a gloomy, overcast morning and as I picked up my books for college I felt that the grey clouds were a picture of the ones hanging over my own life.

I was depressed. However, I was not beyond help; more than willing to try and work things out if I possibly could. My parents were doing all that they could to help. They suggested that I should perhaps go and talk with a counsellor. I willingly agreed and an appointment was made. To be honest, it didn't help me much. I needed more than someone to listen to me – I already had this in my mum and dad. So we went back to my GP who prescribed me with the anti-depressant Prozac. He also referred me to a physiologist at the famous London clinic, The Priory. I was aware that this was where famous celebrities had often gone when they needed help and I believed that if it worked for them, it must be able to help me, surely!

Driving to The Priory I was nervous and unsure of what to expect. The large gothic manor house appeared from around the corner and as we drove up the long smartly kept drive, the frown on my forehead dropped a little. I arrived at the front desk and gave my name to the middle-aged receptionist. She asked me to take a seat in the reception area.

The doctor came about ten minutes later. He was slightly younger than I expected and appeared to be quite a friendly guy. He walked us down the corridor and into his office. It was more like a large sitting room than an office. He had an open fire that was crackling and spitting, and the walls were covered in books, some of which had never been touched. Completing the picture was a rather impressive model of a brain that sat proudly on his desk!

The doctor's respect for me and my feelings was encouraging. We talked for nearly an hour. I remembered him saying: 'Look at me – I'm not much to look at am I? And yet I am one of the most respected and sought after doctors in my field. I'm not perfect and yet I am extremely successful. If it is dependent on looks then I shouldn't be earning the money I am or treating patients like Kate Moss should I?' I knew there was some truth in what he was saying. Without being rude, he was not blessed with good looks, but here he was earning loads of money, happy with his life and respected by people all over the world.

I was referred to a specialist in body image problems that worked on Harley Street in London; his name was Dr James. The doctor felt that this meeting would be of great help to me. He was right. These visits were the catalyst in my process of recovery from the depression that had swallowed my life. He began a crucial process in helping me to help myself.

I recall an early session where he said something similar to what I had been told earlier: 'If you think you have to be perfect before you can be successful in life then you have got things quite wrong. You're missing out on life if you are putting it on hold till you think you're perfect.' Again, deep down I knew he was right.

I attended just over half a dozen appointments with Dr James, sharing my feelings with him for nearly an hour each week. I was slowly beginning to make a recovery and embrace life again.

Despite my depression and frequent doctor's appointments I did quite well in my exams, and so I accepted my first choice place at Nottingham, to study law. But I was still searching for answers both near and far. I decided to have a gap year and to take time to think and experience new things. **I was keen to explore the spiritual as well as the physical**. I took up the Eastern martial art of Tai Chi. It was mysterious and stimulating, something that appealed to me greatly. My parents were excited that I was getting out more and getting involved in normal life again. Dad even came along to the Tai Chi class sometimes. We had great fun together.

As part of my training the opportunity arose for me to travel to Malaysia for a month to train. I jumped at the chance to train with the Masters.

The trip was a great experience but if I was subconsciously looking for truth and meaning in life I was left disappointed; I returned without them. I enjoyed the training though, and continued to practice in the sports fields at Nottingham University. University proved to be a good experience for me. I was given a fresh start; and it was during this time that I became good friends with a couple of people on my corridor who seemed to have something I lacked – they were both Christians.

Jude, a second year, and Kate a fresher, were not how I imagined Christians to be. They were really friendly and interested in others, something that most people I knew were only like during Freshers' Week!

While at times they appeared quite vulnerable I was impressed by the deep strength they seemed to have, something I had never had. 'What should I make of people like this?' I thought, unsure of the answer. It appeared a little strange to me that the two of them seemed so content with God, somebody they had never seen. My mind was closed and unresponsive to their beliefs because they seemed so illogical: this was something for them, but not for me.

A couple of months into university, Kate and Jude persuaded most of my corridor to attend the CU. Kate and some other Christians were going to explain how and why they became a Christian. My corridor friends claimed we were going as moral support for Kate, but really we were all a little curious about the whole set-up.

Kate was a bubbly character, and it was easy to get along with her. I respected her because it was obvious she genuinely believed in God. I sat at the back with my friends listening intently to what she and the others said. The simplicity of it all surprised me. Although each person had different starting points, some of which were really moving, they all came to the same conclusion: they had done wrong against God. As a result of their wrong, or sin as they called it, they had been cut off from having a personal relationship with God.

It is probably fair to say that this was when I really started to consider Christianity as one of my options, tentatively trying to fill the void I felt. It was a decision that made the palms of my hands feel clammy with nervousness. In my opinion Christians were wacky and now I was wondering whether there was something more to them and their beliefs. I asked myself many times: 'Why on earth am I letting myself consider this?' It was because they seemed so normal that I could not dismiss their beliefs totally. I had been taken in by one stereotype already; I didn't want to be taken in again.

Towards the end of the first year I was sort of press-ganged, mainly by Kate and her Christian friends, to attend a group that they called 'Just Looking' which was designed for those who were looking into the claims of Jesus. I was reluctant to go. I was a little embarrassed about attending and really wanted to play football with my friends. In order not to look rude, and partly out of sympathy because I thought few people would attend, I nodded, agreeing to go to the first meeting.

I went along as promised and was pleased to see a handful of others there too. In the following weeks though, football got the better of me and I dropped out of the course.

* * *

The summer holidays or rather summer job as a removals man, was soon over, and I returned to Nottingham for my second year. At the start of term, I was living with three lads and a girl in a small terraced house. My housemates were a good bunch and fun to be around. The guys in particular were larger-than-life characters who were always up for some partying and being lads, keen with the ladies. I went out into town with them sometimes and we had a laugh together, although their idea of fun didn't quite seem to match up with mine any more.

As for most students, term flew by, and before I knew it I was getting invited to Christmas parties left, right and centre. I had always loved Christmas because my family made it such a fun time: time away to recoup your energy levels can never be a bad thing!

Kate and a number of other Christians from my colleges were involved in organising the CU carol service and were keen for me to go. It turned out to be a bit of a house outing. We arrived quite early and were sat about ten or twelve rows from the front. The hall soon became quite full and by the time we had sung the first carol, people were beginning to stand at the back. The candles flickered as 'O Little Town of Bethlehem' rang around the hall. Then a guy was quizzed about why and how he became a Christian. It was similar to the stories I had heard before at the CU. Another carol was sung and the story of Jesus' birth was read from the Bible. Then a little to our surprise, a guy stood up and gave a preachy talk. My housemates weren't too happy about things – this is not what they had come for. I wasn't too bothered though. In fact, the talk was pretty interesting, not to mention entertaining. The speaker's name was Robert and he spoke honestly about what faith in Jesus really means and why we need Him so much. He explained about creation, Adam and Eve, their disobedience and our subsequent separation from God. We were then told about Jesus' rescue plan – His life, death and resurrection so that we might be reconciled to God.

Jesus didn't stay dead though. He came back to life three days later as He said He would, appearing to over 500 people. Before returning back to heaven He made a promise that He would come back just as He left.

I began to fidget. Not through boredom, but because I had so many questions in my head that I was finding it hard to concentrate. Just before Robert finished his talk though, he said something that surprised me a lot.

'I am so glad you are here tonight and have heard about the good news of Jesus. I am going to be standing at the back. If you want to talk to me then I would be delighted to spend time chatting. However, if you need to rush off then my address is on the back of the flyer about Christmas that was on your chair as you came in, and you can get in touch with me that way.'

It was a brave statement – students can be strange people you know! And yet Robert was willing to give us that option, and that impressed me. My friends were ready to leave as soon as it was over. They were bitter that some guy they had never heard of preached at them for thirty minutes.

It took me until the end of the holidays to pluck up the courage to write to him. As I sat down at my laptop and started the letter, I smiled to myself as I realised what I was doing. This was a man I had heard speak once and hadn't even met, and now here I was writing to him, pouring out the questions of life that consumed my troubled mind.

6th January

Dear Robert,

I hope you don't mind me writing to you. I am a student at Nottingham and heard you speak at their CU carol service. I was impressed and would like to ask for your guidance.

My goal in life is to find the truth, or at least strive to find the truth. I struggle to accept Christianity, despite talking with Christians and reading books; I can't divorce myself from the opinion I regrettably feel I am forming – that Christianity is merely a 'self-help' tool.

As I make my journey in life I have found many truths through my experiences, and in this sense I am slowly building myself a centre that has no limits or boundaries. At least this is the view I would like to adopt. Unfortunately, at times my faith in this belief system is significantly undermined. I have nothing greater than myself from which to draw strength, yet this implicitly seems right.

Essentially, I would like to examine the evidence and claims that are the foundation of the belief in Christianity. I would like to be able to feel and know the truth. I have tried praying and have been to the CU meetings. Unfortunately, having experienced various belief systems, I demand more than a supportive role in which my anxieties and problems can be displaced.

I have further reservations, which would certainly be overridden if I could adopt Christianity as the truth. Why is Christianity divided and uncertain? Why does it set absolute boundaries? Why does it condemn practising homosexuals to hell? Why does it take a blanket approach to no sex before marriage, without leaving it to the judgement of the individuals involved? Why does it dismiss all other religions as wrong, without considering the possibility that the truth may have been expressed and interpreted differently around the world? **Was Christianity created in a time of crisis**, suffering and depressions when there was a need for salvation and hope? Is it therefore created by man and impacted on by man's environment?

Yours sincerely and gratefully,

Howard

I licked the stamp and made the short walk to the post box. As I walked home I wondered if I would ever get a reply. I hoped I might, but doubted it. Deciding not to tell anyone about the letter, I put the fact that I had written it to the back of my mind and tried to forget about it.

Three days later my inbox read, 'You've got mail'. To my surprise, I had one from Robert. He was brief but friendly:

Howard,

Thanks for your letter and all your questions. I'm sorry it has taken me a couple of days to reply, but I have been away from my desk.

I am due back in Nottingham in February. I suggest that we meet up for a coffee and chat things through then. Does that sound OK?

Best wishes,

Robert

* * *

In the weeks that followed, preoccupied with exams and coursework, I completely forgot about Robert's reply.

It wasn't until mid-February that I had a strange message from Robert relayed to me by a friend of Kate's. Robert wanted me to know that he was coming to Nottingham in a week's time to speak at a series of evening and lunchtime talks and would I be able to meet up with him after one of the evening talks. I was surprised, to say the least.

Somewhat anxiously I attended the second to last evening talk. I was there with Kate and Andy, one of Kate and Jude's friends, who had given his testimony at the

CU meeting last year. He was really friendly and willing to help explain his faith to me, and as a theology student, I thought he was suitably qualified for the task. Andy and I spoke for a long time that evening during and after Robert's talk. He was very persuasive. Going on the evidence available from the Bible and notable historians, it was, he said, more unrealistic to say that Jesus' resurrection was a hoax than to accept that it really happened.

By the time Andy and I had finished talking, people had begun to leave the meeting and I was introduced to Robert. He remembered me instantly and we made our way back to Andy's house for coffee. Despite a bad cold and a long day, Robert was keen to chat.

As Robert answered many of my questions, he pointed me again and again to the Bible, no matter how difficult I thought they were.

'Howard, the best thing for you to do now is to read the Bible for yourself. As you are a law student, you might enjoy reading the book of Romans.'

We went our separate ways and I was left with much to ponder. My head felt a little less heavy with questions since I was having them slowly answered one by one. It had been a long but beneficial evening, although I was ready to fall asleep as soon as I got home. My housemates were watching a video when I got in, so after a quick 'Hello!' I headed up to my room, falling asleep as soon as my head hit the pillow.

The following two or three weeks were both exciting and challenging. I took out an armful of books from the library that looked at the arguments for and against Christianity. I also did as Robert suggested and tried to read the Bible for myself. I was a little hesitant at first, as I had never really read the Bible before. I started with the book of Mark in the end. What I read was something I had never understood before. As I began to dip into other sections of the Bible I found myself being more and more compelled to believe. It was fair to say that my interest had been aroused – I was now seriously weighing up the implications that this would have on my life.

I had, following the suggestion of Kate, started to attend her happy-clappy church. It seemed a bit mad at first – a lot of singing and clapping and people putting their hands in the air, but I could sense an order and sincerity in it all. A couple of days before what would have been my third visit to church, I felt that deep down things were still not right. I was doing the right thing I guess, by reading the Bible and going to church, but I still knew that I needed to step out in faith to Jesus and receive His forgiveness offered through His death on the cross. I felt I needed to acknowledge Him and was hoping that this week at church, like the other weeks, there would be an opportunity for me to respond.

Sunday morning arrived and I was once again deeply challenged by what I heard. There was nothing new to what the minister was saying; however, this time I knew I couldn't ignore the wrong I had done before God. I needed to ask Him to forgive me and change me so that I might live for Him rather than myself.

Towards the end of the service the minister explained that he was going to invite anyone who had not given their life to Jesus to stand up whilst everyone else had their eyes closed, and he would pray a short prayer. He explained what he was going to say, praying it slowly so that those who were standing could repeat what he had said. I knew I wanted to stand, but I was so nervous that I had to battle to get to my feet. I managed to stand up, my body trembling with nerves, and began to repeat the minister's prayer.

'God, I admit that I have done wrong against you and I want to say sorry. Please forgive me. I want to trust in Jesus who has taken the punishment for my sin. Please will you live within me and change me so that I may become more like you. Thank you for loving me and for hearing this prayer. Amen.'

As I sat in my chair, nothing mysterious or radical happened. However, I did feel a great sense of peace and happiness that I had never experienced in my life before. It was something I now know only comes through having the confidence to say that Jesus has forgiven every wrong I have ever done. Now **with His help I can live for Him every day**, and one day will go to heaven to be with Him forever.

Howard openly admits that the Christian life has not been plain sailing since becoming a Christian, and often has to remind himself that the way he looks and feels has no relation to the peace and happiness that comes from the forgiveness of sins through Jesus. His identity is no longer through his looks, but in the relationship he has with Jesus.

'Don't judge by his appearance or height…The LORD *doesn't make decisions the way you do! People judge by outward appearance, but the* LORD *looks at a person's thoughts and intentions.'*[7]

Naomi

*'The lie continued, the mask parade, as
my soul dissolved'*

Masks: I wore a hundred,
Different colours on different occasions,
So I lived the masquerade.

Underneath: I felt ugly,
Rejected, fearful and scared,
Inwardly breaking.

Mentally: I was longing
To be someone else, to swap characters
In the play of life.

Impression: I was fine,
The lie continued, the mask parade,
As my soul dissolved.

The world: I was angry,
'Beauty' failed to provide me with the lure
Of satisfaction.

Friends: I was frustrated,
Could they not see this despair
Beneath my skin?

Lonely: I was lonely,
Longing for someone to shatter
This pretence.

Searching: I was yearning
For beautiful love, and an approval,
Of who I really was.

Decision time: I was uninterested,
'Religion wouldn't deal, or heal,
With this pain within.'

Change: I was interested!
God told me He loved me and had made me,
Just as I was.

Brokenness: I was shattered,
God's love led Jesus to the cross, where as He died,
He thought of me.

Burdened: I was humbled;
That this was a choice God had made,
To bring me peace.

Called: I was beckoned,
To leave the false behind, live for truth,
For God's praise.

Forgiven: I was forgiven,
Of everything I had done wrong,
My sin was wiped clean.

Accepted: I was loved,
As God's love gradually peeled off,
My masks of illusion.

Healed: I was restored,
From the pain of my insecurity,
Discovering life's purpose.

Decision time: What will *you* do?
Reject? Or accept this relationship
That He offers you?

*Naomi has recently graduated in Social Work from
Southampton University.*

Craig

'It is unlikely that he will ever walk again'

Despite the cold, it was a perfect day for rugby. The ground was still soft from the previous week's rain. There was a little wind drying off the grass and the sun was beginning to shine above the clubhouse. Craig was the captain of his school's 1st XV, playing his usual position of number eight. The annual Boxing Day game was always a highlight in Ballyclare's fixture list. The side were winning; it was going to be a good day. Craig's family were on the sidelines. His dad John was cheering Craig's every move. Rugby didn't really interest the girls too much though; Emma, his sister, and Doreen, his mum were only there to give him their moral support. However, the boredom of a game they hardly understood had got the better of them so they had opted instead to go and chat in the comfort of the family car.

It was then that it happened, in a split second, but it was as if it was in slow motion. The whistle had gone seconds earlier for an infringement; Craig however, who had the ball, was tackled late with a spear-tackle and dumped on to the ground. He lay cold and motionless on the damp grass as worried parents and spectators quickly gathered around him.

Emma and Doreen who were listening to the radio in the car couldn't tell it was Craig so didn't think too much of it as they saw the two teams trudge back wearily to the changing rooms. It was as the guys passed their car that Emma realised Craig was not in the middle of them all where he would normally be, laughing and joking.

'Where's Craig, Mum? He's not with the other guys.'

'He's probably just walking up with your dad,' her Mum replied, as she continued to file the nails of her right hand.

It was then that they saw John running to the car, without Craig. He arrived, breathless.

'Craig's on the ground,' he said. The anxiety in his voice was obvious. 'He's not moving.'

They rushed down to where Craig was lying. His eyes were now open. He was talking slowly to a parent who was gently reassuring him. She was a qualified nurse and was doing all she could to care for Craig. Doreen knelt down beside him, taking his hand in hers. Craig couldn't feel anything.

* * *

Craig was from the small town of Ballyclare, not too far from Belfast. His golf handicap was in single figures and he had representative honours for athletics – sporty only begins to describe his talents. Rugby was by far his favourite sport though. For three years prior to the accident Craig was involved with the Ulster Schoolboys. His dreams of playing for Ireland one day were not unattainable.

His mum and dad were both committed Christians, so from the day he was born John and Doreen had taken him along to Sunday school.

'What the Sunday school was teaching me might sound harsh and overreactive to some, but at the age of five or six **I knew that what they were saying was right**.'

As Craig sat on the beanbag in his Sunday school room, his teacher Mrs McKenzie was explaining how Jesus came into this world so that all who believe in Jesus could be saved from the punishment they deserve for the wrong done against God. She read five short sentences from the Old Testament that rang round in Craig's six-year-old mind: 'It was our weaknesses He carried; it was our sorrows that weighed Him down. And we thought His troubles were a punishment from God for His own sins! But He was wounded and crushed for our sins. He was beaten that we might have peace. He was whipped, and we were healed!'[8]

That evening, as Craig played in his room he couldn't get the thought of Jesus dying for him so that he could be forgiven out of his mind. As he got into bed he was restless and uneasy. He knew from what Mrs McKenzie had taught them that he needed to talk to Jesus, thank Him for dying in his place and ask Him to forgive him. That is exactly what he did. 'I remember lying there in my red and blue pyjamas that were a size too small for me praying: "Dear Jesus, I am sorry for doing bad things. Please, will you forgive me? I want to be good like you. Please will you help me change? Thank you."'

'I was quite young at the time and so I don't think I realised the effect of what being forgiven by God meant until I reached high school. There my friends began to question the things I believed, challenging me on the reliability of it all. I explained that without God's forgiveness we would all face a real and lasting punishment for rejecting Him and going our own way. More often than not I didn't have the answers to all their questions, so I would have to be honest and tell them that I didn't; but when I got home I would read my Bible so that I could tell them what it said, and why I believed the Christian story.'

Craig, perhaps because of his sporting ability, earned the respect of his peers for what he believed and the way he stood up for it. He would love to talk about it when his friends quizzed him; but he would try not to shove it down their throats. Rather he would let them see the difference that being a Christian made in his life. Sport was still a huge part of his life, but it didn't dominate him. At the end of the day God gave Craig the ability to play, so he must first of all love God and not the sport he was playing. His love for God was to be a crucial difference in the days, weeks, and months to come.

* * *

The ambulance's siren could be heard in the distance as those huddled around Craig took off coats and jumpers to try and keep him warm. When the ambulance arrived, the seriousness of the situation became apparent. The paramedics decided not to move him; instead they called for assistance from another ambulance.

Emma was so fond of her 'little' brother. Although younger than her, Craig was much bigger, but she kind of liked that! Emma was home for the holidays – a welcome break from her studies at university where she was training to be a nurse. She and Craig were good friends who enjoyed each other's company. Horror thoughts of time spent in hospital began rushing through her mind. Her little brother whom she loved so much – 'Would he be OK? Would he ever come out of hospital? Would he be in a coma for years to come?' The chill of the day was nothing compared to the chilling questions that were infiltrating her mind.

It seemed ages before the second ambulance eventually appeared from behind the clubhouse, with its lights flashing and siren blazing. Craig was slowly and carefully strapped to a stretcher. Once the neck and back brace were fastened he was lifted gently into the ambulance. As it made its way slowly over the uneven field, into the car park and out onto the road, Craig's family gathered his things together then followed behind in their car. A police motorbike was escorting the ambulance to the hospital. Craig's family couldn't think straight. Their minds were cluttered with the turmoil of everything that was happening.

On his arrival at the Royal Victoria Hospital, Belfast, the staff responded quickly. A consultant had been summoned allowing Craig to be taken straight into theatre. Doreen, John and Emma sat outside, numb with shock, totally speechless. News filtered out to friends and relatives who quickly began to arrive at the hospital. The extent of Craig's injuries was unknown, as tests were still incomplete. It was going to be another couple of hours before they knew any specific details of his condition. The family knew there was only one course of action to take – to pray. Family and friends sat round the coffee table as they began to pray for Craig and the medical staff treating him. Many couldn't hold back the tears as the seriousness of the situation began to dawn on them all.

It was three o'clock in the morning before the doctors were able to give a detailed assessment of Craig's condition. As the consultant came into the room, Doreen could tell it was not good news. He sat down to explain the situation. 'Craig is comfortable, but unconscious at the moment. His injuries are extremely severe. **Craig has broken his neck** and has completely severed his spinal cord. **It is unlikely that he will ever walk again**. He will be paralysed for the remainder of his life. **I am so sorry**.'

Doreen broke down and fell into the arms of her husband John. He was unsure of where to look. It felt as if he had been punched and was now severely dazed. The doctor had brought them the news that they had feared most. As he stood in his crisp white coat, he explained that he would be back shortly to explain a little more of the situation, and with that he left the room. John's mind was flooded with questions, 'What would happen now? Why Craig? Would he be able to...?' He couldn't bear to contemplate the future – the questions were too big, and at this stage there were no answers. He began to realise how totally helpless he was in this situation and there was nothing he could humanly do for his son. **All he could do was pray**, and so as they sat there stunned by the news they had heard, they began to talk to God.

'Lord Jesus,' John said quietly, 'I don't know what to pray, but you promise to be with us no matter what, and so I ask that you will keep your promise and be close to Craig now. Take away any pain he may have and give the consultant and his staff wisdom as they treat him. Jesus, help us to understand what to do. Help us to trust you. Thank you for hearing this prayer. Amen.'

Craig lay in traction for three days. Unfortunately, its success was only minimal. The medical team were forced to look elsewhere for answers. An operation was the chosen option. Rods would be inserted into the neck in order to stabilise it. It was crucial that preparation for the operation was quick. There was a problem though – on the morning of the operation, Craig developed a high temperature. They would have to monitor the situation; if it wasn't down by one o'clock that afternoon, it would have to be postponed. The staff told John and Doreen the situation and once again they began to pray with the friends and family that were with them. To their relief and thanks, by lunchtime Craig's temperature had dropped sufficiently and the operation was carried out as planned.

It appeared to have gone well, but there were many critical days spent in intensive care after it. The greatest problem for Craig now was his breathing. At one point one of his lungs collapsed. The problem was now so acute that a tracheotomy had to be performed to help improve his breathing. These were trying days for Craig and all his family. Emma found it particularly hard at night – thoughts of her brother lying motionless in his hospital bed consumed her mind.

It was January 5th, ten days after the accident that Craig began to show the first sign of improvement. Moving his eyes across to his mum he asked her to tell him what *exactly* was wrong with him.

Trying to say it calmly and softly she said, 'Son, you have broken your neck. The doctors think that you will be paralysed to some degree for the rest of your life.'

Craig still motionless, bit his lip, closed his eyes and said nothing.

Before long Craig's situation was known throughout the Irish rugby community, and he received hundreds of cards and letters from well-wishers he had never met or heard of before. Well-known international rugby players frequently came to visit him and encourage him in his recovery. When a group of Christian rugby players in South Africa heard of his situation they started to pray regularly for him.

It was six weeks before Craig could be moved to a specialist hospital to aid his recovery. His family were by his side as he was transferred to Musgrave Park Hospital to help him settle into his new surroundings. They were not prepared for what they saw. The rows of wheelchairs lined up in the corridor tugged at Doreen's heart. The future held something very different from what she had previously imagined. She couldn't hold the tears back anymore. She tried her best to hide them from Craig, but as they began to roll down her face it became a difficult task. Typically though, Craig thought of things differently. In the time since the accident he had decided that **the future was in God's control**, and that whatever that was, he would accept it. He would enter his programme of physiotherapy and occupational therapy not with fear but great enthusiasm.

On 1st March, Craig's eighteenth birthday, he sat up for the first time since Boxing Day. It hurt him a little, but the excitement of this major development was written all over his face. From here on he made steady progress. His parents came, at his request, to read the Bible to him each evening. Two short verses were of special comfort to him: 'Be still and know that I am God' and 'Cast all your anxiety on him because he cares for you.'[9] Friends at school often wondered how a God who loved Craig could let this happen. His answer was simple: 'It is important to understand that we cannot always explain why certain things happen. However, I do believe God is in control. He knows what will happen to me each day, even before it happens. So to look at it simply, I can be confident in the fact that I know God loves me and that He holds the future. With these two aspects, I have nothing to fear.'

After a couple of trial weekends at home, Craig was finally discharged from hospital at the end of July – seven months since the Boxing Day rugby match. Life was different from what he knew before entering the hospital. He was now confined to a wheelchair unable to play the sports he loved. Craig's attitude and outlook however, stayed pretty constant. Whilst the future would not be easy, he had the confidence that came from his relationship with Jesus: 'Be strong and courageous. Do not be afraid or terrified…for the Lord your God goes with you; he will never leave you or forsake you.'[10]

These words have been a great comfort to Craig. He can testify that 'He has not broken His promise yet. Despite all that has happened, He has never left me and so with His help I will continue to trust Him in all that I do.'

Craig completed his A levels and now studies Construction Engineering Management at the University of Ulster in Jordanstown. His dream to play rugby for Ireland recently came true as he was selected to play for the Irish wheelchair rugby team.[11]

Nick

'They suffered simply for being Jewish'

The humidity of a typical day in Borneo was oppressive. As I sat reading on my bed the perspiration gathered rapidly on my forehead. I was there during my gap year, teaching English to local people at a college in a rainforest clearing. From my room I had extraordinary views of Mount Kinabalu and the surrounding jungle; every day seemed to bring new experiences of life in the tropics – weird sounds and strange creatures. But despite all the excitement of a completely different place and culture, I couldn't get away from my internal anxiety: had my life actually been heading in the right direction for the past three years?

* * *

My family upbringing wasn't Christian at all; in fact I was brought up to be Jewish. Every year my family would celebrate the Passover, which involved a long meal with all kinds of traditional foods like dry, crisp 'unleavened' bread.[12]

When I was thirteen I had my bar mitzvah.[13] You're supposed to recite to the whole synagogue a passage from the Tanakh, the Jewish Bible. On top of that you've got to recite it in the original Hebrew – and you're actually supposed to sing it rather than simply read it! I objected to the singing side of things and thankfully my father let me off that particular requirement. Looking back I can't understand why I didn't take the whole process more seriously. I didn't really ask questions such as: **'Who is this God I'm worshipping?** What kind of control does He have over the world? How does He want me to live? At the end of the day, is He real?'

I went through with it partly to please my father, but also because I was keen to align myself with my Jewish ancestors who suffered not only under the Egyptians, but also under every civilisation since. My great grand-mother died under the Nazis. My great-aunt survived her imprisonment in a concentration camp by hiding up a chimney to avoid being sent to the gas chamber. They suffered simply for being Jewish. I wanted to honour their memory by standing unashamedly for their beliefs.

So as I left for boarding school shortly afterwards I certainly considered myself to be Jewish; but I didn't take the spiritual side seriously at all. I never read the Tanakh. In fact, my one memory of getting the Bible off the shelf when I didn't have to take it into a RE lesson was when my friends and I wanted to see what it would be like to smoke tea. We didn't have any cigarette papers, so we thought Bible paper, being so thin, would be a good substitute. I guess that shows what I thought of God, if I was prepared to treat His book like that.

Instead of caring about God, I was interested in sneaking into the nearby town on a Saturday night with my friends to get drunk, and meeting as many pretty girls as possible through parties and balls.

But during my first three years at boarding school – that time of drinking, partying, smoking and GCSEs – there was one major issue on my mind. I couldn't stop thinking about death. I knew that I, along with everyone else, was going to die, and it seemed to make everything I was doing ridiculous and pointless. I couldn't work out why it was worth lifting a finger to do *anything*, since in the end I'd die, and who'd care about what I'd done with my life then? It seemed ridiculous to me that people put so much effort into their lives when they knew they would die. Living life seemed to me to be like writing a book with ink that fades into nothingness as soon as it dries. Why write the book if the ink is shortly to disappear? Why put so much effort into living life when death makes all that effort meaningless?

As I sat at my desk in my room at school my mind kept fast-forwarding to my death at some moment in the future. It was as if Death in his black-hooded cloak was looking at me and laughing, saying, 'There you are, working away at your French vocab…why bother? You're going to be mine before too long and your French verbs won't be much use to you then will they?'

The band Limp Bizkit wasn't around at that time, but there's a verse in their song 'Take a Look Around' which sums up the way I was thinking:

'Does anybody really know the secret?
The combination to this life and where they keep it?
It's kind of sad when you don't know the meaning.'[14]

I'd have agreed with that 100 per cent. I was desperately aware that I didn't know the secret to this life, and that not knowing it was making me sad. There were some weeks when I shuffled miserably through everything I had to do, without finding the slightest pleasure in any of it, because I didn't 'know the meaning'.

So that's where I was, aged fifteen.

* * *

In our year group assembly one day, a couple of sixth-formers stood up to advertise that night's meeting of the Christian Forum. I was desperate for some kind of explanation, something that might somehow trump death and give my life meaning. So I went along, I thought it was worth a try. The speaker gave a talk on this sentence from the Bible: 'The Son of Man must be lifted up, so that **everyone who believes in him may have eternal life**.'[15]

In other words (as the speaker spelt out to us), when Jesus was lifted up on the cross to die, He opened up the way for God's people to have eternal life. By taking the punishment for their wrongdoing He gave them the opportunity to live forever. I remember the speaker saying: 'There's a great divide between mankind and our Creator caused by our rebellious attitude against Him. But through Jesus,' he continued, 'God has bridged the divide so we can get back into the relationship with Him which we were originally made for – a relationship lasting for ever.' I was faced with a choice: either to trust in God's Son or carry on rebelling against Him and face His punishment.

Eternal life! It was exactly what I was looking for. And I didn't need to become a monk, I didn't need to go on a barefoot pilgrimage somewhere; all I needed to do – according to that verse from the Bible – was to believe in this person called Jesus. The speaker explained that believing in Jesus meant trusting in His solution to the problem of our rebellion against God. He said that true belief in Jesus leads to a willing submission to Him as the commanding Lord of your life.

As the talk ended, I went bounding over to the speaker with a huge smile, but also one remaining problem: 'Yeah, this sounds great, but I've got a bit of an issue because I'm Jewish which probably means I shouldn't believe in Jesus.'

'No that's not a problem,' I was told, 'Jesus himself was Jewish. He's the Jewish Messiah, the one that the Jews were waiting for down the centuries. I've got a friend who's a Jewish Christian, and he says he is a Jew who has found his Messiah. Jesus Christ actually means Jesus the Messiah.'

And that was all I needed to hear. I could still be Jewish; I would not be breaking the family line of Jewishness in which I was glad and proud to stand. I could be a Jew who believed in Jesus as the Messiah, and eternal life would be my reward. **Why delay?** That same evening I prayed a prayer of commitment to Jesus suggested to us by the speaker.

Looking back, I didn't really know what I was letting myself in for. I was so thirsty for eternal life that I didn't pause to think through all the implications of following Jesus for my lifestyle. It didn't sink in that true belief in Jesus must lead to listening to Him as the risen King, and living life His way. I thought I'd done some kind of deal with God to sort out my eternal future, and in the meantime I thought I was free to live pretty much how I wanted. This went on for about two years. The terrible side to this was that I was telling friends and family left, right, and centre that I'd started to follow Jesus, but they saw no impact being made on my life. No wonder they weren't interested in what I was saying, when they saw in front of them the same arrogant, argumentative and self-centred person that I'd always been. Even the drinking and flirting kept their place.

But in my third year, this situation began to change. I went to a conference for sixth-formers run by an organisation seeking to establish links between the Christian Forums of boarding schools like my own. The idea was that we would be encouraged in our faith through meeting other Christians in a similar situation to us. It was exactly what happened. Spending time with them was like breathing a different kind of air – air filled with joy, hope and profound meaning and purpose. I remember doing some Christmas shopping shortly after the conference. I found myself looking with real concern at some other shoppers, as they travelled up a department store escalator. It seemed to me that the life they were all living was worthless and utterly futile compared to the life offered by Jesus.

More to the point, the conference also set me straight in the area of my general behaviour. I was taught the three 'Gs' of the Christian life: the Glory of God, the Good of others and my own Growth as a Christian. 'You should make sure,' I was told, 'that your decisions and lifestyle measure up to the three Gs.' This teaching helped me to see my life from God's point of view – was I really bringing Him glory when I got drunk in full view of my sister, who knew I'd recently become a Christian? Had I given much thought to the good of others when planning my gap year? Had I properly recognised my own crying need for spiritual growth?

I wish I could say that things actually changed in practice from that time on. But with me it seems to take ages for truth to get from my head down to my heart. It was only in my gap year that I faced up to the question that should have been sorted out right at the start: Was I really prepared to make Jesus the Lord of my life as well as my Saviour? To live the way He wanted me to live, rather than simply going my own way with a bit of Christian stuff mixed in now and again? Jesus says, 'If you try to keep your life for yourself, you will lose it. But if you give up your life for my sake and for the sake of the good news, you will find true life.'[16] When He talks about 'giving up your life', He doesn't mean martyrdom but rather giving up your right to call the shots in your own life. Jesus wants lives to be lived totally for Him and in the service of His message of good news.

I remember sweating this out in my room in Borneo. What would this really be like, living wholeheartedly for Jesus? Was I really up for this? Had my life actually been heading in the right direction for the past three years? I remember thinking about the life of a church leader I had got to know in Wimbledon. He lived for Jesus – and he wasn't a monk bound up in a cloister mumbling Latin morning, noon and night. No, he had friends and enjoyed their company; he read novels; he played squash and tennis, he watched the latest films... clearly, I thought to myself, Jesus is not a tight-fisted Lord who holds back pleasures from His people. In fact this same church leader had pointed out to me that when a person lives wholeheartedly for Jesus the colours of their personality shine out more brightly, rather than turning into a uniform Christian grey – which was a fear I had.

As I weighed up the pros and cons of living for Jesus, I found myself struggling with major doubts as to whether or not Christianity was actually true. I didn't want to know if it was merely a nice idea. I had to be totally convinced that it was true. I remember thinking: 'Either I'm a follower of Jesus, on my way to eternal life with Him in a place more glorious than I can imagine, or I'm an accidental collection of bones, blood and cells stuck in an unpleasantly hot part of an unplanned globe in a meaningless universe.' When I thought it through, I desperately *wanted* Christianity to be true, but wanting it to be true wasn't enough. It actually had to be *the truth* before I was willing to live it out.

While all this was going through my mind, I suddenly remembered hearing a talk at school about the resurrection of Jesus from the dead – about the empty tomb which no one could account for; and the way Jesus had appeared to hundreds after his death, appearances which had the effect of turning previously devastated followers into impressive ambassadors for the faith. I'd been thoroughly convinced then of the firm evidence that **Jesus *did* rise from the dead**. And all this came back to me. It was the evidence which I needed to be sure that Christianity was true, and so I joyfully decided to keep on going.

As I was thinking through all of those things it was a great help to meet some of the local Bible-believing Christians in Borneo. The ones I met came from the Dusan tribe, and most of them had never once left the island. Yet they fully believed that the Jesus we read about in the Bible is the risen Lord of all creation. I discovered their experience of following Him was the same as mine – they had also found living His way to be a life of joy, hope and meaning. Jesus had promised that repentance and forgiveness of sins would be preached in His name 'to all nations'.[17] These Dusan believers were fulfilling that promise right before my eyes!

I wouldn't want to end this without saying that living for Jesus has often been difficult. I can think of three difficulties that seem to be impossible for real followers of Jesus to avoid. The first is fighting sin. If you're serious about making Him Lord of your life, which you have to be if your faith in Him is genuine, then you've got to be ruthless with all the evil impulses that emerge from the human heart. That's *hard*. Sometimes I catch myself thinking the foulest things, but they have such a twisted appeal to me that to thrust them out of my mind is more than I can do by myself – I'm forced to cry out for God's help. Being serious about sin means constantly being on guard, keeping an eye on what my mouth is about to say for example. By nature I'm a thousand miles from where God wants me to be so it always takes effort and prayer to live His way. It still doesn't come easily after being a Christian for some time.

Then the next new difficulty that I've had to face is the unpredictable response of those who aren't Christians. Beforehand I'd adapted to fit in with any crowd of people for the sake of popularity, but Christians can't do that. If you're following Jesus then His commands come first, which can often put you on a collision course with the rest of the world. Sometimes I have to put up with the most irrational and cruel treatment from non-Christians, which is obviously deeply hurtful.

The last thing that's difficult is the effort that I have to put into spreading the news about Jesus, and helping new believers to grow up in their faith. On one level I love it, it's incredibly fulfilling and it supplies meaning to every aspect of life; but at the same time it's hard work, and it often brings me to the point where I'm saying, 'This is too much, I really can't go on.' Some of the toughest times I've ever had have been spent as a volunteer leader on Christian summer camps. They can be a case of one gruelling demand after another. But God is always faithful, and as the Bible promises, He supplies the strength I need.

So as I look to the years ahead in this life, I'm certainly aware that they will not be at all easy. But that doesn't put me off for a minute because I consider these years as my opportunity to serve Jesus, the Messiah. He is the one that my fellow Jews have been waiting for throughout their history, and He's arrived, and I know Him and follow Him! He is infinitely wise and kind – He never asks His servants to do anything that is not in their best interests. Serving such a Messiah is what we were designed to do. And at the end of the day, whether it's fantastic or deeply challenging, following Jesus is living in line with *the truth about the world* – what could be more sensible than that? My Messiah is real.

Adam

'Hadn't evolution disproved the Bible?'

To be blunt, Adam's family were well-off. His dad had hit the big time as a chief executive of a large firm in the early 80s. A true businessman if ever there was one, he was an experienced wheeler-dealer, involved with anything from managing night-clubs, to selling reversing cameras to help lorries reverse! In the eyes of Adam and his friends, his father was cool, well respected and to be followed. And so, from his earliest memory, it was on this model that Adam based all his hopes, dreams and beliefs.

'I wanted to be like my dad. **I wanted to be rich; to meet a girl and fall in love and to be care free and live happily ever after.**'

Adam's dad would often give him advice that he would thankfully soak up. While travelling in the car one afternoon, returning from a shopping trip, the conversation swung on to the topic of death and dying.

'Adam,' his father rounded off, 'whatever you do make sure you have fun while you can because this is the only life there is. There is no God, no afterlife. Make sure you live this life up.'

For once though Adam couldn't agree. Thoughts swirled round his head: 'Surely there must be something out there? It seems a little arrogant to say that I am the only thing in this life that is important. There must be someone in control of this world. There must be a God – but does He really hide Himself in the pages of the Bible? What about evolution? Hadn't this disproved the Bible?… Ah well, if God *is* out there and He wants me to do something, I'm sure He will be in touch.' And with that Adam left the thoughts of God and the afterlife to one side and carried on with the combined emotional pressure of adolescence and GCSEs.

Until, that is, he met his old friend Max.

* * *

Adam's GCSEs had passed, the summer was gone, and he was beginning to discover the night-life in his local town as he started out on his A levels. One typical Friday night he bumped into Max, who Adam had not seen for quite a while. Max and his mates were a lot of fun to be around and the group of them ended up most weekends together.

'Max and his mates went to a youth club every Sunday night and asked if I wanted to go. I considered myself to be slightly too old and too cool to be going to a youth club, but in the boredom of a dull middle-class town it seemed a good way to spend a usually quiet Sunday evening. Plus, I started to be pretty good mates with Max and the others – they were a good laugh. I thought I would go along and see what went on.'

So that Sunday, Adam joined Max and the others at the youth club. As they walked through the building Adam couldn't help but allow his eyes to wander around the room.

'I remember thinking, "There are God quotes everywhere!" It all seemed a little weird to me, not realising that in the coming weeks my world-view was about to fall down like a house of playing cards.'

After a strong coffee and a few rich tea biscuits one of the youth workers, Bjorn, came out with something that blew Adam's mind.

'I don't believe that evolution is true.'

'Ha!' Adam blurted out, thinking to himself what an idiot the guy was. 'Everyone knows that evolution is true; it has been proved – it's a fact.'

The discussion was started and Adam was confident of his position. After all, he had done very well in his maths and physics exams, and was now doing A levels in these subjects – he was going to be a force to be reckoned with.

'To my surprise I was losing the argument. The points that Bjorn was raising were ones I had never considered before. He kept referring back to what the Bible said. I couldn't argue with him – I had never even read it. I was a little embarrassed that my confidence in what I thought was fact was so quickly shown to be misplaced.'

Each week Adam went back, keen for an argument. Perhaps he had picked it up from his dad's personality, but Adam enjoyed a challenge, and the spiritual contest at the youth group was a challenge he was willing to rise to. Each week though, Adam was finding that his strongest arguments and opinions were being demolished. Not necessarily by the eloquence of Bjorn and others, but by the sheer weight of evidence that they had through what the Bible said.[18] Even though he was only sixteen at the time, he knew from his own life experiences that what the Bible was saying about him and this world was true.

The Bible says, 'The sinful nature is always hostile to God. It never did obey God's laws, and it never will. That's why those who are still under the control of their sinful nature can never please God.'[19] Adam only had to watch the news to know that this was true. No news programme was needed though when it came to realising this in his own life: he knew full well that he was hostile to God.

'Right,' Adam thought to himself one evening as he and Max drove home, 'if this stuff is true, and I have no reason to think it is not, then I had better go and have as much fun as I can now before I start following God. I need to get the partying done before the boring Christian stuff kicks in.'

And that is where Adam found himself as he started university.

* * *

'When I arrived at Loughborough University I knew that the claims of Christianity were true. However, that didn't mean that I wasn't fighting it. I'll think about following Jesus seriously when I'm a little older, I thought, when the party is over and I'm too old for clubbing, drinking and having a good time. University would only come round once for me – and I was determined to live it and love it.'

Not long into his first term however, Adam was feeling a little disappointed with the life that he thought university days offered. Sure, there were the all-nighters in Freshers' Week and the odd night in town in the weeks that followed. However, contrary to what he had thought, Adam learnt that university was not the non-stop party he was expecting. Instead, he was finding himself to be a little lonely but most of all bored.

'Everything this world promised me had in reality delivered so little. The fast car, extreme sports, drugs, women, money or a stunning holiday all provided brief periods of happiness – but it never lasted. I couldn't figure it out; it didn't make sense to me. I thought it was these things that would satisfy my longings for happiness. I was left disappointed.'

While at home one weekend, Adam received a text from Bjorn.

> Ad – what are you up tonight? Fancy coming to church with me? Let me know. B

Out of courtesy and obligation Adam replied:

> Yeah OK. Pick me up and I'll come!

Adam put his mobile down, a little surprised at the invite but appreciative of the fact that Bjorn had thought to invite him.

'I felt awkward. I hoped no one would talk to me. The praying and singing made me feel a bit uncomfortable but the talk in the middle was quite thought-provoking.' These were Adam's initial reactions that he then put towards the back of his mind.

* * *

During that summer Adam became a regular attender at church with Bjorn.

'Church was good. I guess that surprised me to some extent. I wasn't sure of what to expect, but I did hope that it would leave me with some food for thought – which it did. The guy speaking talked about the same things as Bjorn had at the youth club. The more I heard, the more uncomfortable I felt. Not because I disagreed with it, but because I knew it was true.'

One night as Bjorn and Adam sat together near the back of church, they were reminded of the problem this world has. Adam let his mind flick back to the news broadcast he had seen the previous night. 'You don't need to tell me this world has a problem,' he thought, 'I know it has.' The speaker continued to explain that this was because of sin. 'This is the world's biggest problem' he said, 'but this is also my biggest problem and your biggest problem.'

'We all have this problem – we rebel away from God and go our own way. The Bible calls it sin.'

There was a sense in which the speaker was looking directly at Adam. Adam was all too aware of his sin. At the youth club he had come across the Ten Commandments – 'Do not lie, do not be jealous, do not crave after things that don't belong to you...'[20] He knew that he hadn't done as God had wanted. One day he would face the consequences of hell – a place designed to justly punish those who have deliberately continued to reject God, preferring to live for themselves.

The speaker told of another alternative – the removal of our wrongdoing from the eyes of God. This was something Adam knew all too well from what he had heard at the youth club.

'**Jesus Christ came into the world to save sinners from God's eternal punishment.** The Bible says that "without the shedding of blood, there is no forgiveness of sins."[21] This is why Jesus died. As a result we can have a relationship with God because our sin is no longer standing between us and Him. We still sin, but it is forgiven, and that is where real happiness comes from. The Bible says that those who have been forgiven by Jesus will join God in heaven because their sin has been removed by Jesus' death and resurrection. This is real life that does not come from this world, but from the forgiveness that God offers through Jesus.'

Adam sat there fighting, trying to ignore what he had heard. He was gripping the seat tightly, absorbing every word that was being said – knowing it was true but battling to accept the consequences of believing it. Over the next six months Adam became more and more convinced it was the truth, but was not ready or willing to give up his party life, or to alienate himself from his friends or family. Slowly but surely though, he found that all the things the world offered were becoming less and less satisfying. Deep down, he knew there could only be one winner. He had done wrong – he wasn't denying that. He longed for happiness. He knew his sin was making his life a misery and if he didn't do anything about it he would face the consequences alone, and forever.

'I couldn't put it off any longer. Nowhere else had I had the truth revealed to me by people who weren't out for what they could get, but who were genuine, loving people who cared where I would spend my eternity.'

So, in his second year of university, Adam stopped fighting what he knew was true.

'At the point which I became a Christian there was no sudden crescendo of learning; there was no emotional hype or manipulation. I had recently arrived back from a great skiing holiday in the French Alps and was having some time by myself. As I lay on my bed I started to reason things through in my head. I knew I could no longer be an atheist, or even an agnostic. Evolution had been appealing, but it was only a theory. Could I believe in an accidental big bang that started all life off? This seemed ridiculous the more I thought of it. What the Bible says was true and as a result I had to do something about it. I knew that there was purpose to this life. So I took a step of faith and prayed, what was a clumsy prayer, but I prayed and asked God to forgive me. I had found the truth; finally I had meaning and purpose to life.'

'Being a Christian brings true peace and contentment. I have never once regretted the day I turned from my sin and accepted God's gift of forgiveness through Jesus. Life hasn't suddenly become easy and sometimes it is difficult, but I wouldn't swap it for anything else.'

Tom

'I cannot remember what it is like not to be epileptic'

Tom's eight-year-old life was turned on its head while he was living in Hong Kong. He had been a reasonably healthy, happy-go-lucky kid, who had a huge desire for fun and adventure. However, one afternoon in the cool of an air-conditioned hospital Tom and his family were told their lives would never be quite the same again.

Epilepsy is a severe disorder of the nervous system that causes unpredictable loss of consciousness and convulsions. The convulsions or seizures come in two sorts: the first, commonly known as Complex Partial Seizures (CPS) is a short seizure that lasts for twenty to thirty seconds. The second is quite different, lasting anything between 45 minutes to an hour. The effects of epilepsy are not only unpredictable but the cause is usually unknown too. Faced with the diagnosis, all Tom and his family could ask was 'why?'

Tom's family spent one more year in Hong Kong after Tom had been diagnosed. But for the next ten years Tom's condition did not improve but worsened. His seizures were regular, violent, and absolutely exhausting. At their peak, he was having up to 250 short seizures a day, and one or two hour long ones too. It seemed his body was losing a fierce battle and no matter which drug the hospital would give him, things didn't improve for quite some time. The hospital operated on Tom, inserting a Vagal Nerve Stimulator to try and calm his nerves.

'**I hated the world.** My teenage life was cluttered with disruption, confusion, tiredness and the inability to be independent. I cannot remember what it was like not to be epileptic. I was unable to play sport, learn to drive and swim. I was constantly relying on others: I couldn't go anywhere on my own – my life at the time felt hollow and empty. But why me? I had been a fairly good person. What had I done to deserve this? I would work myself up until I was wrapped in hate. I needed a release from the cage that epilepsy had built around my life.'

Tom had questions, and wanted the answers. He didn't believe there was a God. If there was, surely he would have stepped in before the diagnosis, or cured him of his epilepsy. For Tom, pain and suffering equalled the lack of a supreme controller, an absence of God.

'At one point or another, everybody asks the question "Why am I here and what will happen when I die?" Certainly this was the question on my mind as I started university at Bath. What was the point of *my* life? Surely there must be some reason for living out there, some overriding purpose to it all?'

These questions had governed Tom's mind for a few months now, and he wasn't prepared to leave them unanswered. So with some degree of determination, he hit the university library. Checking out a dozen or so books, Tom was well equipped, hopeful that he would find the answer in at least one of them. When he got home, piling the books on top of the desk, he logged onto the Internet, allowing the search for an answer to grow.

For the next six months, this routine continued. Tom was not leaving a stone unturned. He had a scientific mind, and so approached each religion, idea and theory in turn. What was the scientific explanation? Buddhism, Hinduism, Sikhism; hours were spent weighing up the beliefs and whether or not they were credible – but for each one he was left disappointed. Still he didn't have a logical answer to his biggest question, **'Why am I here and where am I going?'** Discouraged and disappointed, he began to wonder whether he was ever going to find the answer.

It was then that he started looking at the claims of Jesus. Checking out some more books from the library, and buying a couple more from the Christian Union, Tom spent many nights reading into the early morning, grappling with what Christianity was all about.

His seizures were still not under control. Tom was given two carers to ensure that his seizures didn't harm himself or anybody else. They were a constant reminder to him that life wasn't as it ought to be; prompts in his mind to ask 'why?'

'I had seen a number of posters around campus advertising lunchtime talks hosted by the CU. They looked quite interesting, but they also had a free lunch, so I thought I would go along and cash in on the food! As I sat and listened, what the speaker said suddenly seemed to make sense. I knew I had done wrong; I knew the world was in a mess, but was there *really* a God? Did He really create the world or were we here as a result of a big bang? Why, if Christians were special were they so hypocritical? And what about people such as murderers – could God really forgive them?'

Feeling bold, Tom thought he would go and talk things through with Dave, the speaker at the event. Tom left twenty minutes later, with a number of small issues sorted in his mind. However, the big questions remained unanswered. 'I'll come back next week,' he thought. 'I'll get a free lunch, but there is a different speaker next time. I'll see if he can shed any more light on the complexity of it all.'

The following Monday Tom was there, as planned. The lunch was good, and the talk was helpful, but there were still daunting, unanswered questions. He spoke to the speaker again. Twenty minutes later Tom left feeling confused much the same as before, but this time with a little more to ponder. The speaker for the week, Roger, had given him a new piece of advice. 'Tom,' he said, 'if you really want to know more, then the best thing for you to do is this: go to a church that teaches the Bible; read your Bible; and read as much stuff from the CU as you can. Tom, the Bible says, "Ask and it will be given to you; seek and you will find; knock and the door will be opened to you. For everyone who asks receives; he who seeks finds; and to him who knocks the door will be opened."'[22]

Tom left this second lunch much like the first, although slightly more excited about the prospect of finding an answer. 'If I keep looking for God and find the answer, then I know that the Bible is true', he thought. 'However, if I keep looking and don't, then I know it's a bunch of well-written stories.'

The next eight months were an exciting time for Tom. His epilepsy was still not under control. The doctors had explained that it might not ever be now. But the excitement was stemming from the discoveries he was making about the Bible and what it said. He started going to church as the lunchtime speaker had suggested, and he was finding it a great help. It was unlike anything he had done before. The songs were unknown to him, and he didn't know where to start when it came to reading the Bible. However, he kept with it – continuing, as the speaker had said, knocking on the door, seeking for the answer. **It was a puzzle slowly but surely it was coming together.**

'On the way out from church each week, I would pick up a different flyer on issues such as 'Why does God allow suffering?' and 'How can I know the Bible is true?'. They were really helpful and taught me a lot about what the Bible said. I guess by this point I was becoming more and more convinced that what the Bible said, and what Christians believed, was true. They seemed to have things sorted. Not in an arrogant, know-it-all way, but they had a deep understanding of who God was and what relevance He has in the twenty-first century.'

By this time Tom had started to meet with a group of Christian friends he had met at church, to study what the Bible said. He still had doubts and questions and was a little scared of the answers, as he started to realise that he had a responsibility before God as to how he lived his life. Tom's knowledge of what the Bible said was now quite broad, and he knew as much as he needed to know really, but it was all head knowledge. Up until now it had been an academic exercise – something to stretch his mind, but that was as far as he had let it go.

'Things changed dramatically for me in the February of my third year. The CU were hosting a week of events to allow people explore the claims of Jesus a little more closely. Halfway through the week, Roger, the guy who was speaking, challenged people to take a step of faith, to turn an academic exercise of exploring and investigating the Christian faith into a relationship with God that changes your whole life, and eternity.

'**I thought he was talking directly to me.** I had held back and held back from asking Jesus to forgive me for the wrong in my life. I knew that it was only through asking Him to change me and help me live for Him that my life would have real meaning and purpose. We were designed to live in a relationship with God, but sin had cut us off. The Bible had given me the answers to the questions I was asking. I could do nothing but accept it.'

That night, as the meeting finished and people sat chatting and drinking coffee, Tom and Roger got talking.

'Roger, I know it's all true. I know that it is my sin that has cut me off from God – I want and need His forgiveness. I want Him to give me purpose to my life, through His awesome power to change my life. I want to be sure that when I die I will be going to heaven because God has taken my sin and dealt with it for me.'

Roger was delighted. Eight months ago, he had told Tom to explore the Bible further. Tom had done that and found out for himself that it was true. After talking further, Tom prayed: 'Jesus, please forgive me, change me and help me live differently as you would want me to live. Thank you for showing yourself to me over these last few months. Amen.'

Once more, Tom's life was turned on its head. Not with the devastating diagnosis of epilepsy this time, but with the wonderful change that happens when Jesus forgives.

Tom's epilepsy is still not under control, and he is still shadowed by two carers. But there has been a great change in his life and the answer to his biggest question has been answered. 'From my experience, purpose in life comes from knowing God personally, having His forgiveness and living for Him.'

Eileen

'I was a religious hypocrite'

Eileen was brought up like most children in Ireland – as a Roman Catholic. She and her two brothers, Sean and Mike, lived in the beautiful, rural countryside of County Kerry. 'Famous throughout the world for its people, culture and immense beauty, Co. Kerry was a lovely place to grow up,' she recalls. 'Our house was surrounded by meadows, usually containing sheep or cows, and so playing out in the evening with my two brothers was a lot of fun.'

Eileen was a hardworking, diligent young girl who was always keen to show kindness to those around her. Her brothers were both intelligent, especially Sean. Despite her sensitive nature though, Eileen was not a soft touch. At a young age she was fully aware of the chaotic, needy and broken world that she was part of. She was determined to change it, or at least do all she could to contribute to the slow process of turning things around for those who were hurting from the pain caused by this world. As a member and committed participant of the local Social Action Group (SAG), Eileen's life was kept fully occupied with helping others.

Week after week, Eileen struggled to concentrate in Mass. Her numb body from hours sat on a rigid pew reflected something of the numbness of her brain as she tried to work out the issues that were being raised in her mind.

'Mary must be important if she gave birth to Jesus, but why do we need to pray to her? And what about all the saints – what is so special about them?' For a young teenage schoolgirl, studying in a convent school, the barrage of questions was too much. Despite all Eileen's grappling and pondering, they remained unanswered.

She was genuinely interested in religion – the idea that there was a God. Eileen got on well with her teachers, some of whom were nuns. 'On one occasion one of them asked me if I would consider becoming a nun; however I tried to break it to them gently that the idea of not getting married and having children was not one I wished to entertain!'

'Praying to all the saints, as we did, seemed somehow insufficient – they were good people, but just people at the end of the day. **Why couldn't we pray directly to Jesus?** These questions led me to think through seriously where I was heading spiritually. At this time I had a growing sense that I should be praying only to Jesus – after all, the Bible says: "For there is only one God and one Mediator who can reconcile God and people. He is the man Christ Jesus."'[23]

* * *

University College, Cork (UCC) is one of the largest universities in the Irish Republic, with around 12 000 students. Eileen arrived to study a three-year Social Science degree that was then followed by a postgraduate course in Social Work. Despite the outward confidence and satisfaction that she had reached university to study what she had always dreamt of, inwardly Eileen was struggling. The mounting insecurity of her low self-esteem and an escalating anxiety that came with it began to spiral out of control. 'The struggles I had with self-esteem had been brewing for a number of years, but now they were at a head. The majority of them though were, I guess, ones that many girls of that age face.'

Her appearance toyed in her mind for months. While on the whole she was content with the way she looked, Eileen wanted a small change here and there which, slowly but surely, began to eat away at her thoughts. Without realising, the battles in Eileen's head were pulling her down emotionally. She had moved from a loving small country school to being one of thousands on a growing university campus. She was no longer *someone*, but one of many; she was now just a statistic.

As Eileen entered her second year at UCC she moved into a cute, red brick, three-storey terraced house with five other girls, one of whom was Wendi, a 'born-again' Christian. Wendi, from Donegal, was a talented musician who played the flute and violin very well. Despite the hours of music that filled the house, she and Eileen soon became close friends, deciding to share the large loft double bedroom. 'She was a diligent worker, which suited me, as we would both sit at our desks working, keeping each other company. But what I was really drawn to was her kind nature. Wendi's loving person-ality seemed to come as a result of her strong faith in God – or that's how she explained it. Her devotion and concern for others was obvious. It really made me think.'

'Over the coming year Wendi's life spoke volumes to me about what it is to *really* know God. From my earliest memory I can remember being religious, but what Wendi had was not just religion. It was something very real with God – something I had strived after, but had never attained.'

Eileen made a conscious decision to spend more time with Wendi, partly out of curiosity to find out more about her relationship with God. If you were friends with Wendi, you were friends with Peter, Wendi's boyfriend. It wasn't a bad thing in Eileen's mind. In fact, they got on pretty well. He shared the same beliefs as Wendi, which added to Eileen's intrigue. From her point of view, it was one more person she could quiz about God.

The three of them, over that year, became strong friends. 'Looking back, I think Wendi and Peter learnt virtually everything about me. I almost felt it necessary to explain my life and feelings to them, as I wondered if God would care for someone like me. I told them everything, hoping that they could tell me if they thought He would.'

Because of this honesty, Eileen told Wendi about difficulties she had had with her self-esteem in the last year and the continuing battle it was. Wendi's face formed a concerned frown but soon turned to a smile. Her face reflected her personality – she was a girl who was concerned for others and willing to help them in any way she could.

Wendi reached for her Bible – it was the size of an A5 piece of paper and was worn around the edges with use. The spine of the book was battered and the front cover was torn.

'I think you need a new Bible!' Eileen said releasing a little tension from the air after opening her heart to Wendi.

'You're not wrong there!' Wendi replied looking up and smiling, understanding that I was a little uneasy after all I had explained.

Wendi opened her Bible and after flicking over a couple of pages she put her finger about halfway down the page, leaned over so I could see what she was pointing to, and began to read:

'You saw me before I was born.
Every day of my life was recorded in your book.
Every moment was laid out
before a single day had passed.'[24]

'I sat there on my bed, allowing my brain to process what I had heard. The penny was dropping. I was beginning to realise that if God was real – which I believed He was – He created me, loved me and had a plan for my life. That, as Wendi explained to me, was why Jesus died. God had a plan for me that He had written down, even before I was born. I had done wrong against God, but He had a plan, a solution, specifically for me, Eileen!'

'Every day...recorded...every moment...laid out...' The words Wendi had read to Eileen were ringing in her ears. She was unable to let them go.

This was the beginning of a long conversation between the two girls that covered all aspects of life and religion. However, Eileen's mind wouldn't rest. As she walked to the bus stop she caught herself smiling. Despite worrying that those around her might think she was weird, she continued grinning, wondering what it was that was making her smile.

'As I let my mind work through all that Wendi had told me about God's love I couldn't help but smile. She had told me some great news that I could and should be excited about. After years of praying it was not until now that I committed my life to Christ and had reason to be smiling about whom God was and His concern for me.'

'I had been a religious hypocrite. I didn't need Mary, or a good attendance at confession or even Mass, but what I needed was the forgiveness of Jesus, God's Son – the only One who could bring me into a real relationship with God, just as Wendi and Peter had.'

* * *

Anxieties and fears sometimes still grip her, but remembering her conversation with Wendi, Eileen knows that **God has a perfect plan for her life** and that she can totally rely on Him. He has not let her down yet. In Jesus Eileen has found identity and purpose to her life.

With heartfelt experience she can say with confidence, 'It is only the love, mercy and grace of God which can meet the most heartfelt and intimate needs of people today. I do not regret putting my trust in Jesus one bit – **it has been the best decision of my life.**'

The Truth

Jesus said, 'My purpose is to give life in all its fullness'[25]

Whether you're a girl wondering, 'Does this top look OK?', or a guy asking his girlfriend, 'Where is our relationship going?' we want the truth. Forget the politician's answer, we plead, just tell us the truth!

What is the truth about Christianity? What is it all about? Are Christians overzealous religious nuts, insane fanatics who have done more harm than good, or is the God they follow really who they say He is – the Saviour of the world?

Uncovered

After spending a couple of years with His disciples, Jesus asked a group of His closest friends, 'Who do people say that I am?' They gave a flavour of the various opinions that were circulating at that time. Then Jesus asked, 'Who do you say that I am?'

Peter, the most outspoken of Jesus' followers immediately replied, 'You are the Christ.' He had recognised that Jesus was the One who had been promised in the Old Testament Scriptures for centuries, the One who would save the world.

Jesus explained to His followers why He had come. He said, 'I must suffer many things and be rejected by the elders and chief priests and scribes, and be killed and after three days rise again.'[26]

As this book has shown, Jesus continues to change lives by bringing people into a living relationship with God. He is still the person in history who cannot be shaken off, still a figure that generates interest. Take for example the interest there was in the film *The Passion of the Christ*. Millions follow Him, not out of compulsion, but with love and trust.

To answer Jesus' question as to who He really is, is to answer one of the most fundamental issues there is. What can be more important than investigating the claims that Jesus is God?

Firstly, the Bible says that **He is the Son of God** and so we should listen to Him. Parents, friends, lecturers, billboards, e-mails, the media; there are so many voices demanding our attention, that to some extent we chose which world we live in. Like Phil or Umesh you might think that Christianity has some credibility, but want to live for the moment. Or like Adam you may think that you are good enough to get to heaven on your own. The voice of God the Father still remains: 'This is my Beloved Son, hear Him!'

Jesus came into the world as a baby, grew to be a child, a teenager and then an adult that He might reveal God to us. God became a man and lived here on earth, in the person of Jesus. By looking to Him, we can see exactly what God is like in the way Jesus acted and reacted to life's challenges.

Jesus is the example above all others of how we should live in a world that has been ruined by wrongdoing and is in rebellion against God. Ultimately, Jesus came to die as a sacrifice for us. Through His death, He was paying the penalty for all our wrongdoing and so fulfilling all the

Old Testament prophecies concerning His suffering and death on the cross.

Seven hundred years before Jesus was born Isaiah wrote:

> 'He was despised and rejected, a man of sorrows, acquainted with bitterest grief.
>
> We turned our backs on him and looked the other way when he went by. He was despised, and we did not care.
>
> Yet it was our weaknesses he carried; it was our sorrows that weighed him down. And we thought his troubles were a punishment from God for his own sins! But he was wounded and crushed for our sins. He was beaten that we might have peace. He was whipped, and we were healed! All of us have strayed away like sheep. We have left God's paths to follow our own. Yet the LORD laid on him the guilt and sins of us all.
>
> He was oppressed and treated harshly, yet he never said a word. He was led as a lamb to the slaughter. And as a sheep is silent before the shearers, he did not open his mouth.'[27]

Yet death was not the end. Through His resurrection, Jesus gained victory over Satan's great trump card: death. Jesus rose again from the dead and for those who believe, is now our sympathetic representative in heaven. We may speak directly to God because of what Jesus has done for us.

A prison chaplain once became a prisoner for a few days in order to be able to identify with the people to whom he was ministering. He desired to understand all that they were experiencing. Jesus Christ, as God in coming to this earth in humanity was 'God with us', identifying and empathising with our needs and wants.

Of course, there are those who deny that Jesus is God. The Islamic faith is passionate about who Jesus is not, as well as who they believe He is. Jehovah's Witnesses or Mormons who are frequently found knocking on the doors of our homes, don't believe Jesus is God. However, if Jesus Christ is not God, then God is guilty of misleading us, because in His Word, the Bible, we are encouraged to transfer our affection from ourselves to the creator. The Bible tells us to love Christ, to follow Christ, to imitate Christ, to trust Christ and even to worship Him. Surely we would not be commanded to worship a mere mortal.

Secondly, **Jesus is the Man of God**. Jesus was as much a man as any man is, as well as being as much God as God is. He knew what it was to be tempted in every way that we are, and yet He was sinless. He was mocked, but remained bold and fearless in all that He said and did. He was hounded by His enemies, but remained courageous, and steadfastly set His face to going to Jerusalem where He would die and rise again. He was tested and questioned and yet always remained humble, but firm. He was determined, out of love for us, to go to the cross and die. The Bible says that 'God was in Christ reconciling the world to himself.'[28] You can read more about Jesus' life in one of the gospel accounts.

As a real man, Jesus was tempted. He also knew what it was to be hungry, thirsty, tired and lonely. Yet He never had to apologise or blush with embarrassment or shame. He was totally innocent. Despite all of this He was rejected by the people of the day. In fact the Bible says, 'Even in his own land and among his own people, he was not accepted. But to all who believed him and accepted him, he gave the right to become children of God.'[29]

Thirdly, **Jesus is the Lamb of God**. Throughout pre-Christian times Jewish believers who recognised their wrongdoing would take an animal to a priest so that the animal may be sacrificed. It took the penalty of the individual sinful person's wrongdoing. And yet an animal can't really take away human sin. Every sacrifice was picturing the fact that eventually Jesus Christ would come and would die taking on Himself sin and death.

Jesus came to die for Tom, Kate, Howard and the others; he came to die for you and for me. He died so that our sin that cuts us off from God, our wrongdoing, might be forgiven and removed, in order that we can enjoy full access and intimacy with God.

Finally, **Jesus is the way to God**.

Jesus said, 'I am the way, the truth and the life.'[30] There is only one way to God and it is not by us trying to reach up to Him. God has taken the initiative in coming to rescue us. He took the first step in reaching down to men and women and rescuing us. Whoever we are, whatever we have done or whatever our background, Jesus Christ is willing to forgive us if we ask Him and come to Him.

Whether you can identify with Kate, Craig, Tom, Adam or any of the others – whatever our background, the only way to God is through Jesus and what He has done.

As all of these stories testify, Christians are not all they should be or indeed what they want to be. To quote Kate, 'I still struggle every day to make the right choices…as every Christian does, but God has stuck to His promise…He *has* heard me every time I have cried out to Him.' However, Jesus has done a work within us, not only to forgive the past, but to help us day by day until one day when in heaven everything will be made new, including sinful Christians. He promises to be with us throughout eternity. God promises that those who have trusted Him as their Saviour will not go to the hell they deserve, but to heaven, which is God's gift given to those who turn from that which is wrong and trust Him.

Uncovered. Fact/fiction, truth/lies. You decide. Will you ask Jesus to become your Lord and Saviour of your life? Many have found that praying similar words to these have helped them in coming to know real forgiveness:

'Heavenly Father, I confess my sin to You and I want to turn from it. Please forgive me. I trust Jesus as my sin-carrier, my Lord and Saviour of my life. Please come to live within me. Help me to become more like You and follow You more closely. Thank you for loving me and hearing this prayer. I pray in Jesus' name. Amen.'

If you would like help in starting to live as a Christian, or would simply like to discuss the issues raised in this book, please e-mail Jonathan at carswell77@aol.com

Further Reading

Christianity Explored, Rico Tice and Barry Cooper (Carlisle: Authentic, 2001)

Fresh Start, J.C. Chapman (London: Hodder and Stoughton, 1986)

Real Lives, D.J. Carswell (Milton Keynes: Authentic, 2004, reprinted)

Testing Darwinism, Philip E. Johnson (Leicester: IVP, 1997)

The Relationships Revolution, Nigel Pollock (Leicester: IVP, 1998)

Turning Points, Vaughan Roberts (Carlisle: Authentic, 2003, reprinted)

Why Believe? Roger Carswell (Milton Keynes: Authentic, 2004, reprinted)

Why Should God Bother with Me? Simon Austen (Tain: Christian Focus, 2002)

Notes

[1] John 14:6.
[2] *Fresh Start*, J.C. Chapman (London: Hodder and Stoughton, 1986).
[3] 1 Corinthians 6:9.
[4] Mark 2:1–12 (NLT).
[5] Psalm 34:15–19 (NLT).
[6] Romans 10:9.
[7] 1 Samuel 16:7 (NLT).
[8] Isaiah 53:4–5 (NLT).
[9] Psalm 46:10; 1 Peter 5:7.
[10] Deuteronomy 31:6.
[11] Craig's story first appeared in *Life Times* magazine. Some of the information above came from that article and has been used with permission.
[12] The Passover is a celebration remembering the rescue of the Jews from slavery under the Egyptians. This took place over 3000 years ago.
[13] The bar mitzvah is the religious initiation ceremony of a Jewish boy who has reached the age of thirteen; the equivalent for boys of confirmation in the Church of England.
[14] 'Take a Look Around' features on Limp Bizkit's album *Chocolate Starfish and the Hot Dog Flavoured Water* (Interscope, 2000).

[15] John 3:14–15.
[16] Mark 8:35 (NLT).
[17] Luke 24:46–47.
[18] For a more in-depth look at the creation/evolution debate, see Philip E. Johnson, *Testing Darwinism* (Leicester: IVP, 1997).
[19] Romans 8:7–8 (NLT).
[20] For all ten of the commandments see Exodus 20:1–17.
[21] Hebrews 9:22 (NLT).
[22] Matthew 7:7–8.
[23] 1 Timothy 2:5 (NLT).
[24] Psalm 139:16 (NLT).
[25] John 10:10 (NLT).
[26] You can read this account of events in Mark 8:27–38.
[27] Isaiah 53:3-6 (NLT).
[28] 2 Corinthians 5:19.
[29] John 1:11–12 (NLT).
[30] John 14:6. See also 1 Timothy 2:5–6.

Real Lives

by D.J. Carswell

'You are on a train; you look at the people around you. Someone hides behind a newspaper. Another dozes; a young man nods to the beat from his Discman. A baby cries further along the carriage and a table of football fans celebrate an away victory over a few cans of lager. Someone's mobile goes off; a student sitting next to you sends a text message. Eavesdropping on the conversations you catch soundbites from those around you. Who exactly are they, you wonder?'

Real people.
All different.
Everyone with a life story.
Real lives.

In **Real Lives** you will meet, among others … a famous footballer … a sophisticated lady from South Africa … an Olympic athlete … a backpacker exploring the States … a Brahmin from India … a young, abused girl … the greatest man in history who was a child refugee … and the author's own story of a changed life.

ISBN: 1-85078-412-4

Available from your local Christian bookshop or www.WesleyOwen.com

Turning Points

by Vaughan Roberts

Is there meaning to life? Is human history a random process going nowhere? Or is it under control – heading towards a goal, a destination? And what about my life? Where do I fit into the grand scheme of things?

These are topical questions in any age, but perhaps particularly so in a largely disillusioned postmodern era such as ours. Vaughan Roberts addresses these questions and others as he looks at what the Bible presents as the 'turning points' in history, from creation to the end of the world.

This book does not read like a normal history book. No mention is made of great battles and emperors of whom we learnt at school. It will not help you pass exams or score extra marks in a pub quiz.

It aims to do something far more important, to help you see history as God sees it, so that you might fit in with his plans for the world.

'Racy and profound, brilliant and biblical, this book is a powerful apologetic and magnet to Jesus Christ.'
Michael Green, Adviser in Evangelism to the Archbishops of Canterbury and York

Vaughan Roberts is Rector of St Ebbe's Church, Oxford. He has worked extensively with students and is a frequent speaker at University Christian Unions, and at conventions such as Word Alive and Keswick. He is a keen sportsman.

ISBN: 1-85078-336-5

Why Believe?

By Roger Carswell

Why Believe?

... the Bible is the Word of God?
... the Devil is the Enemy of God?
... the World is Alienated from God?
... Jesus is the Son of God?
... Death has been Defeated by God?
... Christians are Children of God?
... Jesus is the Only Way to God?

All of us need to tackle these issues.

The Leeds-based evangelist, Roger Carswell, offers clear, concise, and compelling answers to all these questions, without dodging any objections. And he shows how the puzzled 'Why believe?' can be transformed to the confident 'I do believe.'

ISBN: 1-85078-079-X

Available from your local Christian bookshop or www.WesleyOwen.com